Agile Documentation

Agile Documentation

A Pattern Guide to Producing Lightweight Documents for Software Projects

Andreas Rüping

JOHN WILEY & SONS, LTD

Other Wiley Editorial Offices

John Wiley & Sons Inc., 111 River Street, Hoboken, NJ 07030, USA

Jossey-Bass, 989 Market Street, San Francisco, CA 94103-1741, USA

Wiley-VCH Verlag GmbH, Boschstr. 12, D-69469 Weinheim, Germany

John Wiley & Sons Australia Ltd, 33 Park Road, Milton, Queensland 4064, Australia

John Wiley & Sons (Asia) Pte Ltd, 2 Clementi Loop #02-01, Jin Xing Distripark, Singapore 129809

John Wiley & Sons Canada Ltd, 22 Worcester Road, Etobicoke, Ontario, Canada M9W 1L1

Wiley also publishes its books in a variety of electronic formats. Some content that appears in print may not be available in electronic books.

Library of Congress Cataloging-in-Publication Data

Rüping, Andreas.
  Agile documentation : a pattern guide to producing lightweight
documents for software projects / Andreas Rüping.
      p. cm.
  ISBN 0-470-85617-3 (Paper : alk. paper)
  1. Flexible manufacturing systems. 2. System design. I. Title.
  TS155.65.R87 2003
  005.1'5–dc21

                                  2003011756

British Library Cataloguing in Publication Data

A catalogue record for this book is available from the British Library

ISBN 0-470-85617-3

Typeset in Garamond Light and Frutiger by WordMongers Ltd, Treen, Cornwall TR19 6LG, England
Printed and bound in Great Britain by Biddles Ltd., Guildford and Kings Lynn
This book is printed on acid-free paper responsibly manufactured from sustainable forestry,
in which at least two trees are planted for each one used for paper production.

Contents

Foreword

As Jerry Weinberg says in his classic text *The Psychology of Computer Programming*:

Documentation is the castor oil of programming. Managers think it is good for programmers, and programmers hate it! The value of documentation is only to be realized if the documentation is well done. If it is poorly done, it will be worse than no documentation at all.

Nothing in the Agile Manifesto (`http://agilemanifesto.org/`) states 'Thou shalt not do any documentation', but since many developers have a genetic reluctance to any form of writing that isn't expressed in a programming language, they have clasped the following principle to their collective bosoms:

...we have come to value: Working software over comprehensive documentation

and proclaimed to the world that documentation is out.

My software development career has been mostly on large projects, like the one that developed the software for the Boeing 777. There is no way that projects like that can dispense with documentation. I would be the first to admit that the 777 project and all the others I have seen close up could have been done better. They could have been completed just as well in a less ponderous fashion. Not only do I believe that there's always room for improvement, but I also believe that we should strive continually to improve – especially on safety-critical projects. So either we admit that projects of this magnitude are hopelessly 'non-agile', or we agree that, when it's appropriate – that is, when it adds value – there is a need for documentation. I vote for the latter.

Now, however, we're faced with the dilemma – what does that mean on an agile project? Can a project really follow agile principles and still produce documentation? This is the question Andreas Rüping addresses in this book. Andreas has documented his experiences of successful and unsuccessful project adventures with documentation. He shares an array of encounters with diverse projects: small to large, old technology to new, spanning the past 12 years. I've become a believer in the power of stories – nothing is better than hearing what others have done. When we share our successes and failures, we all learn. There are lots of good stories here, real projects all, with some instructive lessons learned and some pitfalls to be avoided.

Andreas does a good job of explaining the trade-offs: when documentation is better than face-to-face, when on-line is better than hard copy, when diagrams are more useful than text. In a discussion near and dear to my heart, he also shows how documentation impacts the customer.

All this information is captured as a set of related patterns. Just like stories, I'm a believer in the power of patterns. I've written many myself and I can attest that they provide guidance in a useful form. Andreas provides sufficient information for us to apply this guidance and benefit from his experience. This is useful, practical stuff.

The book follows its own principles. It is lightweight and presents the useful ideas without burdening the user. It is easy to read and understand and presents solutions that are clearly based on real project experience. I found myself nodding in agreement or tilting my head in consternation as I read something surprising. I learned a lot by reading this little book, and I'm sure you will, too.

Linda Rising

Preface

If you work in the software industry, you will know that documentation plays an important role in many projects. Among other things, documents describe user requirements, software architectures, design decisions, source code and management issues.

There can be a lot of value in such documents. Documentation can contribute to the success of a project by making necessary information available to the team members. Documents can preserve knowledge within a team, and prevent the team from re-inventing things when team members leave and new people join. Documents can capture expertise gained in one project and make it available to future projects. When knowledge has been committed to paper, it cannot be lost.

However, we are living in the information age. We are surrounded by much information, often too much. It can become difficult to filter what we really need. Projects sometimes suffer from too many documents and too long documents. If this is the case, team members looking for specific information can easily get lost. Some things are also much better communicated face-to-face than via written documents. Too much documentation is as bad as no documentation at all.

It is also hard to keep documents up to date when their subjects undergo change. Keeping documents up to date is especially hard when a project is busy and many other things require attention. But outdated documents can easily lead readers onto the wrong track – outdated documents often do more harm than good.

This book takes an *agile* approach to documentation – an approach that is both lightweight and sufficient, in the same vein as the agile approaches to software development that recently have become popular (Cockburn 2001, Highsmith 2002, Ambler 2002).

This book presents a collection of patterns – guidelines that offer solutions to the recurring yet multi-faced problems of documentation. These patterns are governed by the following overall principles:

- Project documentation is most effective when it is lightweight, without any unnecessary documents, yet providing all the information relevant to readers.

- Documents that are considered necessary can only prove useful if they are of high quality: accurate, up-to-date, highly readable and legible, concise and well structured.

- Tools and techniques are useful only if they facilitate the production of high-quality documents and make their organisation and maintenance easier.

- The documentation process must be efficient and straightforward, must adapt to the requirements of the individual project and must be able to respond to change.

It is important to emphasise that this book does not prescribe a standard method that claims to solve all the problems associated with software project documentation. First, such a method is virtually impossible, as no two projects have the same documentation requirements. Second, a heavyweight method is the last thing I would want to propose – a fully-fledged 'standard' documentation method would be too inflexible and would involve too much bureaucracy to be useful. It would certainly not be agile.

This book focuses rather on the elements and processes that can repeatedly be found in good project documentation, and that express an agile attitude. Such elements and processes have been shaped into patterns that you can use to design the documentation that fits your individual project best, and that contributes to the expertise held in your organisation.

Scope
This book is meant for people who work in the software industry and whose job includes writing software documentation at some point. This is true for most software engineers, designers, consultants and managers. If you belong to any of these groups, then this book is for you.[1]

Perhaps you enjoy documentation, or perhaps you see it as a burden. In either case, this book will give you hints on how to focus on what is important in documentation, it should make your documentation process more efficient, and it should lead you to better results.

You can use agile documentation in different kinds of projects. First, agile documentation is targeted at software development projects. Development projects have an overall goal of delivering working software that satisfies the customer's requirements. In a development project, documentation is a means, not an end: documentation is supposed to help the team accomplish their tasks. This book recommends documentation that is as lightweight as possible, but no lighter.

Consultancy projects are also within the scope of this book. Consultancy projects place slightly different requirements on documentation than development projects, since consultancy projects sometimes have documentation, rather than software, as the desired project output. Consultancy projects can profit from an agile approach, as such an approach makes the documentation process more efficient and the resulting documents more compact and straightforward.

Organisation Before presenting the actual patterns for agile documentation, this book begins with some introductory remarks on agile development and on patterns. If you would like to read about the *Agile Manifesto* and how it relates to documentation, this introduction will be useful to you. If you would like to learn what patterns are and how they can be used, you will also find answers in the introduction. A section follows that briefly describes the projects in which the patterns in this book were observed.

The actual collection of patterns is found in the five main chapters of the book, each of which deals with a particular topic of software project documentation. Specifically, the main chapters address the following areas:

1. *Finding the Right Topics*

   Documentation is important: some aspects of a project require documentation desperately, while others do not. So which documents are necessary in your project, and what topics should they cover? What level of detail is

---

1. The book, however, is not about the sort of user manuals that come, for example, with standard software packages, software installation guides or the like, nor is the book targeted at documentation that is produced by professional technical writers.

necessary? What documents are perhaps unnecessary? This chapter presents some guidelines on how to find out what documentation your project requires.

2. *Structuring Individual Documents*

Well-structured documents give readers better and quicker access to information than poorly-structured documents. But what does a document structure look like? How can you make sure your readers easily find the information they're looking for? This chapter offers suggestions about how to increase the readability of project documents.

3. *Layout and Typography*

Readability is one thing, legibility is another. How can document layout support the readers' ability to grasp a document's contents quickly and reliably? How can such a layout be achieved with standard word processors? This chapter tells you how to improve the appearance of your documents easily.

4. *Infrastructure and Technical Organisation*

This chapter talks about how you can manage your project documents. The chapter begins with organisational issues: how can you obtain an overview of the project documentation? Are the documents supposed to be printed on paper? What about on-line documentation, which is becoming more and more popular? Solving such issues quickly leads us into more technical topics: how can documents be processed and stored? How can you make sure that individual documents can be found easily? What steps need to be taken to make project documentation easily maintainable? What tools are necessary for this?

5. *Management and Quality Assurance*

The final chapter addresses management issues such as budget, responsibilities and priorities, as far as project documentation is concerned. The questions to ask here are: what does an efficient documentation process look like, or, how can bureaucracy be avoided? Being agile means putting people in the foreground, so this chapter emphasises the roles people play in the documentation process and stresses the importance of feedback and reflection.

**How to read
this book**

There are different ways to read this book. You don't necessarily have to read
the book in sequential order:

- If you are interested in a quick overview, just go through each pattern
quickly and read the boldface sections. These form thumbnail sketches
that give you an overall impression of the actual pattern. In addition, a
summary of all such thumbnails is given at the end of the book.

- Read the complete patterns if you want to gain deeper insight, and particularly if you're interested in the rationale behind the individual patterns.

- Begin with the experience reports, if you'd like to take a journey through
several real-world projects. The reports explain how the patterns were
used in those projects.

It's a good idea to combine these approaches. You can start with the thumbnails, so you get an overview of what the book has in store, and read the
complete patterns when you become interested in the details or the background of a pattern. You can then use the thumbnails as a checklist when
you work on the documentation of your project, using the complete patterns
when dealing with more detailed issues. Alternatively, you can begin with the
experience reports, and follow the references to the individual patterns
whenever you feel a pattern is of particular interest to you.

If you are interested in some topics more than others, you can concentrate on
the chapters that are of particular interest to you. Pointers will occasionally
refer you to related material in other chapters.

This is a relatively short book: it is intentionally lightweight and aims to
follow the approach it proposes – you don't have to read many hundreds of
pages. Many of the patterns fit on two or three pages, and you can use the
thumbnails if all you need is a short overview. It won't take you too long to
make yourself familiar with an agile approach towards the documentation of
software projects. I'd like to invite you to take this approach with the goal of
making documentation more effective for authors and readers alike.

I am interested in receiving your feedback on this book. If you have any
comments, feel free to contact me at rueping@acm.org.

Andreas Rüping

Acknowledgements

Project thanks

My first ideas on agile documentation (though I didn't refer to it as such at the time) date back several years to a time when I was working at FZI (Forschungszentrum Informatik, Research Centre for Information Technology) in Karlsruhe, Germany. During a few research projects and several industrial collaborations, I had the chance to learn a lot about what characterises good project documentation. But there was more to it than this: the team spirit among the group allowed me to enjoy those years a lot. My thanks go out to everybody in the group, especially Gerhard Goos, Claus Lewerentz, Simone Rehm, Franz Weber, Dieter Neumann, Walter Zimmer, Thomas Lindner, Eduardo Casais, Annette Lötzbeyer, Achim Weisbrod, Helmut Melcher, Oliver Ciupke, Benedikt Schulz, Rainer Neumann, Artur Brauer, Jörn Eisenbiegler, Markus Bauer and Holger Bär.

My understanding of good documentation was refined when, a few years later, I joined sd&m software design & management AG, Germany. I had the chance to look at the documentation produced in several projects in which I was involved. Many of the patterns included in this book came to my attention when they were successfully applied in sd&m's projects. Thanks go out to my colleagues for being a good team, for the fruitful collaboration throughout many projects and for many insightful discussions.

Over the last few years, EuroPLoP – the European conference on software patterns – has been an excellent forum for discussing all sorts of topics around patterns, for me and for others. Thanks to everybody with whom I was happy to collaborate in our efforts to organise the conference, especially Frank Buschmann, Jens Coldewey, Martine Devos, Paul Dyson, Jutta Eckstein, Kevlin Henney, George Platts, Didi Schütz and Christa Schwanninger.

EuroPLoP turned out to be particularly helpful when I submitted papers on various aspects of documentation. First of all, I'd like to thank those who acted as shepherds for my papers: Ken Auer, Ward Cunningham, James Noble and Charles Weir. Their comments and suggestions for improvement had a lasting influence on the patterns that would make it into this book. Moreover, many people offered valuable feedback and loads of good ideas in the Euro-PLoP workshops. They are too many to name in person, but their help was greatly appreciated.

A workshop on 'Patterns for Managing Light-Weight Documentation' at the OT 2002 conference in Oxford also generated helpful ideas. Thanks to all participants.

When I put the manuscript for this book together, several people volunteered to work as reviewers. Scott Ambler, Wolfgang Keller, Klaus Marquardt, Linda Rising, Peter Sommerlad, Markus Völter and Egon Wuchner took the time to read the draft, offered their insight and made valuable suggestions for improvement. This book has profited a lot from their generous help.

Several people have provided a lot of support throughout the publishing process. First of all, I'd like to thank Gaynor Redvers-Mutton of John Wiley & Sons for her work as the editor of this book. She provided a lot of help in making the book come to life. Thanks also to Karen Mosman for her support in the early stage of the publication process, to Jonathan Shipley for taking care of many organisational details, and Juliet Booker for her work as the production editor. Last, but certainly not least, I'd like to thank Steve Rickaby of WordMongers for the smooth ride through the copyediting stage. This was a very enjoyable process that spawned fruitful discussions on the contents, language and layout of the book.

Family thanks I'm happy to acknowledge that this book has also profited greatly from people who weren't directly involved. My final thanks go out to Gerhard, Hiltrud, Jutta, Sven-Folker, Magnus, Nils Johann and Mareike for encouragement, support and those moments of balance that you need when you go through the process of writing a book.

Introduction

Agile development

Agile documentation has borrowed its name from the ideas of *Agile Software Development*. Agile software development was originally proposed by the *Agile Alliance* – a group of 17 software practitioners who first met in February 2001 to collect ideas for better ways of software development.

These ideas are described in the *Agile Manifesto*, which can be found on the Web (`www.AgileAlliance.org`) and which is also cited in a number of books (Cockburn 2001, Ambler 2002, Highsmith 2002).

Here is the central part of what the Agile Manifesto says:

> We are uncovering better ways of developing software by doing it and helping others do it. Through this work we have come to value:
>
> **Individuals and interactions** over processes and tools
>
> **Working software** over comprehensive documentation
>
> **Customer collaboration** over contract negotiation
>
> **Responding to change** over following a plan
>
> That is, while there is value in the items on the right, we value the items on the left more.

The manifesto continues with a number of more detailed statements and concrete recommendations.

Agile development is not one specific method of developing software. Agile development comprises several methods proposed by different people, which apply in different contexts and have different characteristics. All these methods have in common, however, the fact that they are centred on the core values expressed in the manifesto.

Some of the best-known agile methods have been described in books:

- In his book on *Agile Software Development* (Cockburn 2001), Alistair Cockburn speaks about the central role that teamwork plays in software development projects, and about the communication issues that arise in development projects of different sizes and at different levels of rigour.

- Jim Highsmith's book on *Adaptive Software Development* (Highsmith 2000) views software development issues from the perspective of complex adaptive systems. His new book on *Agile Software Development Ecosystems* (Highsmith 2002) gives an overview of the principles of agile development, and includes interviews with several noteworthy figures from the agile community.

- Scott Ambler's book on *Agile Modeling* (Ambler 2002) addresses the modelling part of the software development process. It details practices that lead to effective and lightweight modelling, placing special emphasis on the human aspects of software development.

- *eXtreme Programming* (Beck 2000) was proposed by Kent Beck. XP, as it is usually known, is an agile method centred on programming in its social context. XP welcomes changing requirements and places much emphasis on teamwork.

- Another agile method is *Scrum* (Schwaber Beedle 2001), put forward by Ken Schwaber, Michael Beedle and Jeff Sutherland, who draw on the importance of self-organisation and reflection.

- Mary Poppendieck's forthcoming book on *Lean Development* (Poppendieck 2003) describes a number of principles of lean thinking, targeted at software development leaders.

As the Agile Manifesto is still rather new, we can expect more agile methods for software development to arise in the near future.

The role of documentation

What role does documentation play in an agile project?

The first thing to understand is that documentation appears on the right-hand side of the value statements in the Agile Manifesto. This means, in short, that the best documentation in the world is no excuse if the project is supposed to deliver software, but fails to do so.

This does not mean, however, that documentation is generally unimportant or that documentation need not be provided.

Let's take a look at what the authors of some of the agile methods have to say about documentation:

- Alistair Cockburn recommends that documentation be 'light but sufficient' (Cockburn 2001). He introduces the *Crystal* family of methodologies, which is targeted at projects of different size and criticality. The *Crystal* methodologies require documentation to be created, but let the individual project decide what that documentation should consist of.

- Scott Ambler's book on *Agile Modeling* (Ambler 2002) includes a chapter entirely devoted to documentation. This chapter is named *Agile Development*, just like this book. Scott Ambler's chapter and Chapter 1 of this book were parallel efforts. They follow different presentation styles, but they come to similar conclusions. Scott Ambler compares the agile approach to documentation with 'travelling light': to 'create just enough models and just enough documentation to get by'.

- Jim Highsmith, in *Agile Software Development Ecosystems* (Highsmith 2002), warns us not to produce documentation for documentation's sake, but calls for a balance: 'Documentation, in moderation, aids communication, enhances knowledge transfer, preserves historical information, and fulfils governmental and legal requirements'.

My view is that a light-but-sufficient approach is favourable for two reasons. First, such an approach prevents the project team from expending unnecessarily large effort on documentation. Second, light-but-sufficient documentation is more accessible, and therefore more useful, for a team than voluminous documentation. I think Scott Ambler asks the right question: 'What would you rather have, a 2000-page system document that is likely to have a significant number of errors in it, or a 20-page, high-level overview?' (Ambler 2002)

Certainly, detailed documentation is sometimes necessary, but usually the more concise and accessible documents resonate most among readers. Details often change more quickly than documentation can be updated, and are better communicated face-to-face. (There is more on written, as opposed to face-to-face, communication at the beginning of Chapter 1.)

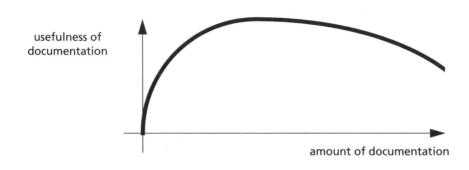

Figure 1. The usefulness of documentation

Figure 1 demonstrates the relationship between the amount of documentation and its usefulness. Beyond a certain point, the usefulness of documentation decreases when more information is added, because finding relevant information becomes more and more difficult as the overall amount of documentation increases.

I think I can summarise this by saying that quality is more important than quantity in project documentation. A certain level of detail and comprehensiveness is necessary – and depends greatly on the individual project – but it is the concise documents that contribute most to communication in a project team. The effort that you can save by producing *light* documentation is better spent on the *quality* of the documents that you do create, making those documents accurate, up-to-date and well organised.

People sometimes get the impression that, in an agile context, not only is lightweight documentation given preference over comprehensive documentation, but also that quality isn't so important. I think this is a misconception, and clearly I disagree. If you decide that a document is necessary, then it must have a purpose, otherwise you wouldn't make the decision to create it. But to fulfil that purpose, a certain quality is essential.

As with so many other things, you can choose to do something or you can choose not to, but if you choose to do it, then it's best to do it 'right'.

The patterns in this book invite you to deal with documentation in an agile way. They don't prescribe a strict process, but offer best practices for defining the right amount of documentation in your project, and for making that documentation flourish.

Patterns

So what are patterns? Let me explain.

This book deals with a variety of questions about documentation. What documentation is necessary and useful? Which topics should be covered? How should individual documents be structured? How can the project documentation as a whole be organised, and what tools are necessary to do so? How can you organise the documentation process?

If you have been responsible for aspects of the documentation of a software project, you have probably faced at least some of these questions. Such questions aren't new – whoever contributes to the documentation of a software project faces them over and over again.

Lurking behind such questions are recurring problems that have recurring solutions. These recurring solutions, or patterns, can be used as guidelines for the documentation of future projects.

A *pattern* in this sense is essentially a well-proven problem-solution pair, presented in a structured form. Users can look up patterns for their particular problems, apply the solutions, and thereby draw on the general expertise available.

In fact a pattern is a little bit more than this. A good pattern also describes the *forces* that are associated with a problem – all those issues that influence or constrain possible solutions. A pattern therefore not only presents a solution, but also offers the rationale behind that solution.

Finally, patterns normally don't stand alone. A single pattern solves a single problem, but when we approach a topic in its entirety, more often than not we are faced with a set of related problems. So what we need is a set of related patterns. The degree to which patterns are related differs. Some collections of patterns are loosely coupled and take the form of a catalogue, while others are more strongly interwoven. In the latter case, we speak of a *pattern language*.

Domain expertise from several disciplines has been described in pattern form:

- The idea of patterns originally emerged from architecture. The architect Christopher Alexander coined the phrases 'pattern' and 'pattern language'. He uses patterns to capture century-long expertise on building towns and houses (Alexander Ishikawa Silverstein 1977, Alexander 1979).

- The idea became popular in software engineering in the early 1990s. The first pattern book to gain much attention was the book on object-oriented *Design Patterns* by Erich Gamma, Richard Helm, Ralph Johnson and John Vlissides – the 'Gang of Four'. This book includes a catalogue of patterns that describe reusable object-oriented designs (Gamma Helm Johnson Vlissides 1995).

- Since the mid 1990s, a book series on *Pattern-Oriented Software Architecture* has covered various aspects of software engineering. The first volume (Buschmann Meunier Rohnert Sommerlad Stal 1996) deals with software architecture in general, while the second (Schmidt Stal Rohnert Buschmann 2000) focuses on distributed systems.

- Jim Coplien has worked extensively on organisational patterns. His *Generative Development-Process Pattern Language* (Coplien 1995) covers the management of organisations and projects, with an emphasis on various aspects of teamwork.

- Martin Fowler's book on *Analysis Patterns* covers requirements analysis and analytical modelling (Fowler 1996).

- *Small Memory Software* by James Noble and Charles Weir offers patterns for software development in a context in which memory resources are limited, such as embedded systems (Noble Weir 2000).

- *Server Component Patterns* by Markus Völter, Alexander Schmid and Eberhard Wolff presents patterns for building server-side component infrastructures (Völter Schmid Wolff 2002).

- Alistair Cockburn's book on *Surviving Object-Oriented Projects* gives an experience account of object-oriented projects and includes a set of project management patterns (Cockburn 1998).

- Mary Lynn Manns and Linda Rising plan to publish a pattern book on *Introducing New Ideas Into Organizations* (Manns Rising 2003).

- More patterns have been created to describe various aspects of software engineering, including analysis, architecture and design, management and teaching. Many have been published through the books in the patterns series (PLoPD 1995, 1996, 1998, 2000) or through the conference proceedings of EuroPLoP, the European conference on software patterns (EuroPLoP 1998, 1999, 2000, 2001).

- Linda Rising published a *Pattern Almanac* that consists of an index to patterns in software and related areas, and which provides a rich list of references (Rising 2000b).

- More resources on patterns are available through the Web site of the Hillside Group (`www.hillside.net`), a non-profit organisation that runs several patterns conferences.

Patterns aren't invented – they are observed. The great benefit of patterns is that they emerge from many people's long-term experience: patterns represent mature knowledge. They describe what has worked many times, which, on the other hand, means that they do *not* describe brand-new scientific results. The patterns in this book have been 'mined' over many years from several projects in which I was involved. They describe the essence of what has worked well in the documentation produced in these projects.

Patterns don't stop here. The patterns community places much emphasis on review culture. The community runs several conferences at which patterns are written, read and discussed. Authors receive feedback on submitted patterns through a so-called 'shepherding' process prior to a conference. At the conference, patterns undergo a sound review process when they are taken to a writers' workshop.[2] Many people offered feedback and shared their insight when earlier versions of the patterns in this book were discussed in such workshops (Rüping 1998a, 1998b, 1999a, 1999b). This book therefore contains the shared experience of many people.

Many of the patterns in this book may give you an 'aha!' experience, because they describe things with which you're familiar. The collection as a whole, however, is new, and should serve you well as a compact guide.

---

2. This review culture has been described in several works: Richard Gabriel's book on writers' workshops (Gabriel 2002), as well as pattern languages about shepherding by Neil Harrison (Harrison 2000) and about writers' workshops by Jim Coplien (Coplien 2000).

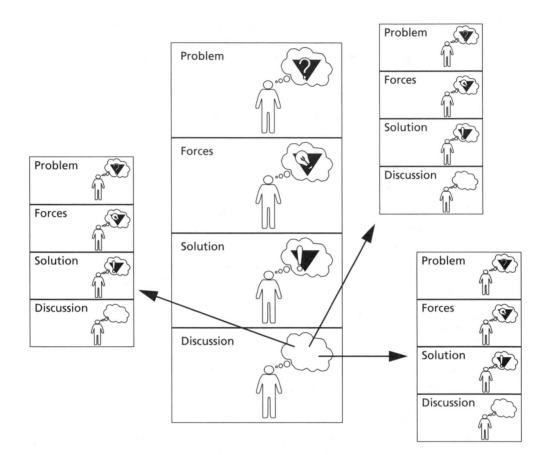

Figure 2. Patterns – guidelines in structured form

Pattern structure

A great benefit of patterns is that they follow a common, structured form that makes them easily accessible – a *pattern form*. The pattern literature has seen many different forms, ranging from more heavily structural to more prose-like forms.

Throughout this book, I use the pattern form illustrated in Figure 2:

- Each pattern begins with a brief problem statement. This statement consists of a question that introduces you into the problem.

- Next is the forces section that motivates why the problem really is a problem. The section describes which forces have an influence on possible solutions. Often conflicting forces tug at possible solutions and build up a tension that the solution will resolve.

- The solution gives an answer to the question posed in the problem section. It begins with a brief statement on how the problem can be solved, and continues with a more detailed description of that guideline.

- Finally, the discussion section gives you some additional information and describes relationships to other patterns – mostly other patterns in this book, although occasionally there are connections to patterns written by other people.[3]

Together, the problem section and the first paragraph of the solution form a thumbnail that makes it possible for you to get an idea of the pattern quickly. The forces section, the rest of the solution and the discussion section offer more detail, background information, and rationale.

---

3. Pattern names of patterns in the book are set in small capitals, while patterns written by other people are set in italics and have a reference to the original source.

Project Background

Before we plunge into the actual patterns, I'd like to take a brief look at the projects from which the patterns in this book were mined. It's a rather diverse set of projects, ranging from software development to consulting, from old technology to new technology, from small teams to large teams. I was involved in most of these projects as a software engineer, project manager or consultant, while for some projects I had a chance to act as a reviewer. These projects were carried out at the organisations I worked for during the last twelve years:

- FZI (Forschungszentrum Informatik; Research Centre for Information Technology), Karlsruhe, Germany, carries out research projects as well as industrial collaborations, with good documentation being a natural part of all projects.

- sd&m software design & management AG, Germany, is a software company that runs projects in various application domains – development projects using all kinds of technology, as well as consultancy projects. Documentation plays an important role at sd&m, with a focus on quality rather than quantity.

The examples I provide throughout this book draw on these real-world projects. The example materials are not taken verbatim from these projects, however, and do not represent the original contents. This was necessary to avoid disclosing proprietary information such as business ideas and software architectures owned by customers. I also had to translate some of the original material from German into English. In addition, I present the projects anonymously to avoid discomfiting any organisations. The topics, structure and purposes of the example documents are, however, authentic.

**Project
Paracelsus**

Customer	A medium-sized German software company
Type	Software development
Topic	Building components for a framework for warehouse management that the customer planned to sell to the pharmaceutical industry.
Technical Basis	UNIX, C++
Size	6 people plus 2 people from the customer's staff
Duration	1 year

This project started off with a specification prepared by the customer that detailed the interfaces the framework components had to implement. The first task for the project team was to come up with a design, which was then discussed with the customer.

In the next stage, the components were implemented and integrated into the customer's framework. Once this was done successfully, the project was considered complete. Later, the customer made a few changes to the components when the framework, of which they now were a part, was used in actual pharmaceutical applications.

**Project
Webber**

Customer	A scientific association
Type	Consulting
Topic	Introducing Web technology to the customer, setting up a Web server and structuring the Web site.
Technical Basis	UNIX, Netscape Server, HTML
Size	3 people
Duration	6 months

This project was carried out when the Web was still new – at the beginning of the 1990s. The customer requested support for setting up their new Web site. The project team and the customer met for a small workshop session, in which the contents and structure of the Web site were discussed. This revealed that the Web site was supposed to mirror the hierarchical structure of the customer's organisation. The team refined the Web site's structure, installed a Web server and launched the site.

After the project was completed, the customer developed the Web site further and maintained the Web server themselves.

Project Extricate

Customer	A medium-sized German insurance company
Type	Re-engineering
Topic	Extracting hard-coded information about insurance products from the policy management system into a database.
Technical Basis	BS 2000, Windows NT, Cobol
Size	8 people plus 4 members of the customer's staff; more people from the customer involved temporarily
Duration	2 years

The goal of this project was to re-engineer a legacy life insurance system to improve its maintainability. This involved a transformation of the data model, and a migration strategy to move the system from the old model to the new one. The functionality was not supposed to change.

Before starting any migration activities, the team had to understand how the old system worked. The team learned from the users and documented what they had understood. Based on this understanding, the team sketched the new data model and outlined the way in which the system should work in the future. The actual refactoring then took place, extracting many of the hard-coded properties into a database.

Project Persistor

Customer	A large German insurance company
Type	Software development
Topic	Building a framework for database access, including application object versioning; introducing the framework into several projects.
Technical Basis	BS 2000, CICS, DB2, Windows NT, Cobol, an OO Cobol extension
Size	6 people, plus 2 people from the customer's staff; about 50 people from 6 other projects during requirements analysis and integration
Duration	2 years; integration with other projects extending over 2 more years

This project was embedded in the larger context of other related projects that together developed several new systems for an insurance company. The goal of this specific project was to provide a database access layer to be used in several applications that were developed by the other projects. The data access layer was designed as a framework, so it could be adapted individually by the projects that would use it.

The project team collaborated closely with the teams who worked on the related projects, in particular during the specification phase and the integration of the data access layer into the applications.

Project Vista

Customer	A large European insurance company
Type	Consulting
Topic	Analysis of the application landscape in the customer's company and the relationships between the various software systems; risk management.

Technical Basis	Various systems, COBOL, C++, Smalltalk
Size	2 people; several members of the customer's staff
Duration	8 months

The customer's organisation operated a large number of systems that implemented many business processes, using a wide range of technologies. Some of the systems were fairly new, while others had been in use for almost twenty years. All these systems worked together, passing data to each other, calling functions and so on. An understanding of the relationships between these systems was important as far as maintenance of the whole system landscape was concerned.

The goal of this project was to analyse the application landscape and to point out risks in the overall architecture.

Project Navigator

Customer	A supplier of automotive software
Type	Software development
Topic	Building a graphical user interface for an automotive navigation and communication system.
Technical Basis	Windows CE; C++
Size	8 people
Duration	1 year

This project developed several user interface components for which the specification was provided by the customer. The components were integrated to form a full graphical user interface such as it is used in the navigation and communication systems found in many cars.

The team designed and coded the components, ensuring that they could be configured to match different 'look and feel' standards. The components were tested under conditions specific to embedded systems.

**Project
FlexiCar**

Customer	An automobile manufacturer
Type	Software development
Topic	Scheduling of automated production steps for time and cost minimisation.
Technical Basis	UNIX, Java, WebLogic Application Server
Size	50 people, including several members of the customer's staff
Duration	2 years

When the project started, the customer already had a clear idea of the expected outcome of the project. Car manufacturing consists of many production steps: the customer was looking for an automated scheduling of these steps, so that the production machines would be used to maximum capacity, and the entire production process would therefore become faster and thus less costly.

The scheduling details were clear to the experts, but the technical implementation represented a great challenge. The team collaborated closely with the customer on a precise specification, and designed the system carefully, taking into account issues such as performance requirements and fail-safety. After the implementation was completed, the customer carried out maintenance of the system.

**Project
AirView**

Customer	A European airline
Type	Software development
Topic	User interface for passenger check-in.
Technical Basis	Windows, C++, Java, CORBA
Size	30 people; several members of the customer's staff also involved
Duration	2 years

The outline of this project was to provide a new graphical user interface for a passenger check-in application. The functionality itself would not be changed. The user interface had to meet certain ergonomic criteria.

The project began with an analysis, carried out with the customer, of the typical use cases. The team then designed some prototypical user interface elements and discussed them with the customer. Once there was agreement over the detailed appearance of the interface, the components were fully implemented.

Project Contentis

Customer	The umbrella organisation of a German industry
Type	Consulting
Topic	Selection of a Web content management system.
Technical Basis	UNIX, XML, HTML
Size	3 people, plus 2 members of the customer's staff
Duration	3 months

The customer organisation was looking for a Web content management system. The project goal was to support the organisation with the choice of a system that would fit their needs. The team's first task was to analyse what these needs were. The team talked to the people who were going to use the system to determine the processes associated with the maintenance of the organisation's intranet and extranet Web sites.

A catalogue of criteria emerged from the process analysis that the content management system had to fulfil. Once the complete list of criteria was established, several vendors were invited to demonstrate their systems in workshops. Based on these workshops, the team made a recommendation of the system that met the customer's requirements best.

Project OpenDoors

Customer	A company in the financial industry
Type	Software development
Topic	Design and implementation of a Web architecture.

Technical Basis	J2EE, JSPs, Servlets, EJBs, Web services
Size	50 people, including several members of the customer's staff
Duration	2 years

The customer intended to create an Internet-based software architecture that allowed them to conduct electronic commerce over the Web. The project goal was to set up a portal through which banks could access information on insurance products and sell such products to their customers.

The project consisted of several collaborating teams. One team worked on the overall architecture, one team worked on the Web content that was going to be presented, and more teams worked on the individual applications that were going to be integrated into the portal. A special emphasis was placed on extensibility, so that the customer could gradually integrate more applications as their business demanded. The teams worked closely together to first create a working prototype of the portal, then to extend the portal and make it more widely available to business partners.

1 Finding the Right Topics

The correct amount of documentation is exactly that needed for the receiver to make her next move in the game.

Alistair Cockburn (Cockburn 2001)

A couple of years ago, a colleague of mine joined a project that had been running for a while. On his first day, he met the project manager, who explained a few things, then handed the new team member a set of documents. Some of those were huge – they contained the entire specification of a complex application. The project manager was visibly proud of the fact that his team had produced such comprehensive documentation. A couple of hours later, I saw my colleague sitting in his office, in front of a large pile of paper, looking rather unhappy. A question about how he was getting on with the project materials revealed that the poor guy wasn't getting on well at all. He said he was "drowning in the specification", and that he couldn't keep all the details in his mind. Eventually he learned many of those details, but more from discussions with the other team members over the next weeks than from reading the documentation.

I remember contrary stories, as well. A colleague, who had just joined the company, was given an introductory document for her first project – a 20-page paper that included all the useful things to know about the project, as well as a list of people to contact for various questions. The colleague later commented that this document was really helpful in making her familiar with the project.

In the first incident, the amount of information was simply too large. The new team member resorted to face-to-face communication, which is what the project manager should have planned in the first place. In the second incident, the brevity of the introductory document and the links it provided were the key to its success.

Claiming that shorter documents should generally be given preference over longer documents is a bit too simplistic, though. I remember a team who had to do some refactoring and were happy that a substantial design document was available, since the original designers were no longer on the project. This document was rather detailed, as it included a discussion of the design alternatives the original designers had considered, and described the reasons for the design they had chosen. The document was of much help during the refactoring, and prevented the team from exploring design options the original designers had already rejected for good reasons.

These stories conjure up the question of why some documents turn out to be useful, while others do not. Apparently some things can be communicated very well through documents, but others cannot. To this end, it is useful to contrast the role of documentation with face-to-face communication. The following table summarises the important characteristics of each.

Face-to-face communication	Documentation
Direct interaction	Self-determined pace
Face-to-face communication allows for quick question-and-answer cycles. You ask something, someone answers, you ask back on a specific detail, you get a more precise answer, someone else offers their ideas and so on. Face-to-face communication involves people in a very direct way.	Different people grasp information at different speeds. Many people find they still have questions when a discussion is over – questions they didn't think of in the heat of the debate. Documents, however, allow people to read at their own pace, going back and forth through the material as they need to.

Face-to-face communication	Documentation
Non-verbal communication People don't communicate through words exclusively. A large part of communication takes place in a non-verbal way – through sound, gestures and subconscious body language. These things are possible only through face-to-face communication.	Introvert communication While some people love to engage in debate, others don't. Introverted people are sometimes painfully silent during discussions, though they may have a lot to say. They have their say more easily when they are given the chance to write things down, as this allows them to have second thoughts and take time to reflect.
Personal involvement Talking to each other means getting to know each other. Building trust happens much faster among people who are in the same room than among people who communicate through writing only.	Scalability Documents can be made widely available. You can address an almost unlimited number of people at a time. Moreover, documents can reach the members of a distributed team – people working in different places.
Fast availability In a well-organised project, there are *Experts In Earshot* (Cockburn 1998) readily available for answering questions you may have. Discussions can come up on the spur of the moment. Documents may be available as well, but time goes by until documents are written and made available.	Long-term availability Once a project reaches its end the team disperses – experts may no longer be available. The software, however, will still need maintenance or even refactoring. Only written documents are available beyond the limits of the actual project.

So face-to-face communication and documentation aren't opposed to each other. Neither is generally better or more effective than the other. Which communication channel is more appropriate always depends on the situation. Either has its advantages, and both complement each other. There are plenty of examples from everyday life. Students learn from books as well as from their teachers' lessons. We learn what's going on in the world around us both from reading the newspaper and from talking to our friends. Neither verbal nor written communication is dispensable in a civilised society.

It's no surprise therefore that projects require both face-to-face communication and written documentation. Exchange of information happens frequently in software projects, and it happens in very different contexts. Agile documentation aims at using the type of communication that best fits such contexts.

So in which contexts is written documentation recommended?

Let's go back to the Agile Manifesto for a moment. The manifesto says that individuals and interaction, as well as working software, are among the core values of an agile development project. We can conclude that documentation is most valuable if it contributes to these overall goals. In this sense, documentation is a means, not an end. The more it helps the individuals in a team interact, the more useful documentation becomes, and the easier it makes it for the team to develop working software.

This at least is true for development projects. In consultancy projects, however, documentation may be the primary goal. Although non-development projects are outside the scope of the Agile Manifesto, we can apply an agile attitude to the documents written in consultancy projects as well.

This book does not promise a fully-fledged documentation method. Projects differ greatly and documentation requirements differ from project to project. Therefore this chapter won't present a list of documents and tell you that these are the documents your project needs. Instead, I have put together several patterns that guide you on your way to defining the specific documentation requirements for your individual project, and determining the necessary contents of those documents.

Figure 3 presents a roadmap diagram of these patterns. It sketches the patterns and the relationships that hold between them, and so gives you a brief overview of this chapter.

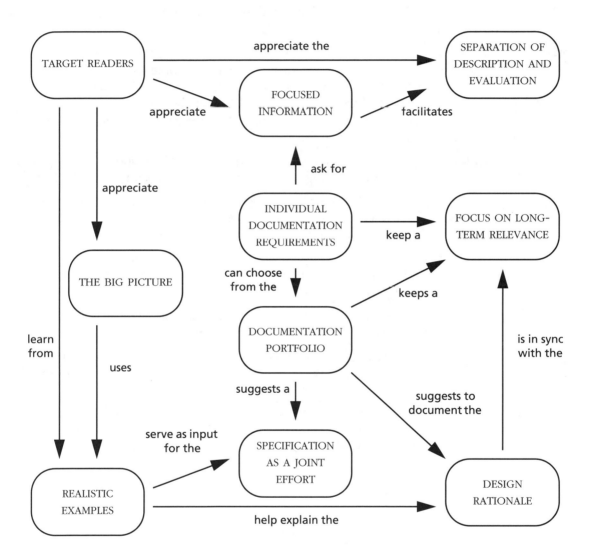

Figure 3. Patterns for finding the right topics

Target Readers

Problem   **How can the project team ensure that the documents they produce will be appreciated?**

Forces   Project documentation addresses many different readers: project managers, architects, designers, programmers and users. People in different roles typically take different perspectives, and are interested in different aspects of a software project. Managers might not be interested in reading a more technical document, even if they are able to understand it, while programmers might not be interested in a management summary.

Moreover, different people often have different backgrounds. Material can be straightforward for some people and difficult to understand for others.

But it's the readers for whom you prepare a project document (Haramundanis 1998). If your document isn't suited to the intended readers' needs, it's likely to be of little or no use.

Worse yet, the very existence of a document is questionable if it is unclear who should read it. If the intended audience cannot be named, what is the point in writing the document?

Solution   **First and foremost, each document must have a target readership, and must address these readers in order to prove useful.**

In an agile context, you don't write a document because a process dictates it. You write a document because that document fulfils a purpose for the intended readers.

The first step is therefore to decide, for each document, who the target readers are. These can be colleagues from the same project, acting in any of the roles mentioned above, colleagues from other projects, perhaps future team members, perhaps customers.

Once this is clear, matching the document to the readers' needs includes the following:

- Making clear who the target readers are by mentioning them explicitly, preferably near the front.

- Explaining what background information is necessary for understanding the document. This can be technical knowledge or knowledge of project specifics.

- Not assuming more background knowledge than can be expected among the target readers.

- Restricting the scope of the document to what the target readers will expect. This helps keep the documentation short and precise, as does restricting the level of detail to what the intended readers can understand.

- Making the document comprehensible by providing examples and other supplementary material from your readers' everyday project life.

When you prepare a document, regard your work as a service to the readers, and therefore keep asking yourself: 'Who are my target readers?', 'What information do my readers need?' and 'What will my readers be able to understand?'

If you conclude that you cannot determine who your target readers are and why they should read your document, there is a high probability that the document is unnecessary.

Discussion   Several other patterns help you implement this pattern. Addressing the target readers has much to do with keeping a focus: the more focused your document is, the clearer can you make the target audience. Presenting FOCUSED INFORMATION helps you stay on target. The inclusion of REALISTIC EXAMPLES and of a GLOSSARY makes it easier for your readers to understand what you're saying.

Certain documents find a large readership easily. For example, overview documents fall into this category – documents that describe THE BIG PICTURE of a software architecture. Because such documents have many target readers, they are useful in many projects.

Becoming aware of your target readers is one thing, addressing them directly is another. The GUIDELINES FOR READERS at the beginning of a document is the perfect place to explain who the target readers are and what background information is required for the understanding of the document.

Sometimes it's hard to imagine what material readers will expect from a document, and what the readers will or will not be able to understand. If you find this makes it hard to define the scope of your document, you can ask others to review the outline of your document. Someone from outside the project can perhaps take A DISTANT VIEW and provide feedback.

Focused Information

Problem

How can documents be prevented from meandering and getting nowhere fast?

Forces

Project documentation as a whole often addresses multiple topics and is typically distributed over several documents. This invites the following questions: in which cases should you opt for separate documents, what material should go into each document, and how long should the individual documents be?

The first aspect worth mentioning is that relatively short and concise documents help keep the project documentation within reasonable proportions. This is desirable both for the project team that has to spend resources on documentation, and for the readers who must access information quickly and reliably.

However, brevity alone doesn't make documents easy to use. Another important aspect is to avoid redundant information. If you let each document cover exactly one topic, you can avoid overlaps between documents to a large extent. This has two advantages. First, a clear focus on one topic makes it easy for readers to identify the document that holds the information they are looking for. Second, avoiding redundant information makes documents easier to maintain and prevents documentation from becoming inconsistent.

Avoiding redundant information also has drawbacks. If, in an attempt to avoid redundancy, too many aspects are extracted into documents of their own, the resulting documents will be less self-contained. Documents will be cluttered with references to other documents, which is counter-intuitive to normal sequential reading.

Solution

A clear and identifiable focus on a particular topic makes a document concise and straightforward. The straightforward document offers the information relevant to this topic, but no more than that.

Related information should therefore go into a separate document if it can be considered to form a topic of its own, while information that is necessary for the immediate understanding of a document should be kept inside it.

Here are some signals that indicate whether a document has a clear focus:

- A document should be aptly titled; a clear title suggests that the focus of the document is also clear.

- The differences in scope between two related documents must be clear from their titles.

- An abstract or summary at the beginning of a document can explain the focus of the document.

- All sections of the document should consist of material that is relevant to the topic the document represents.

You can achieve straightforward documents if you remind yourself to check that whatever you are saying really contributes to the topic the document represents. If you find that this is not the case, go back and ask yourself what the purpose of the document is, and what you intend to convey to your readers.

The consequence of this pattern is that you avoid redundant information to some degree, but not entirely. Small overlaps between documents are fine as long as they are necessary to make documents self-contained.

This pattern doesn't only apply when you set up a new document. Documents evolve as a project goes on, and it's important that they do not evolve into a verbose mass of text, growing beyond reasonable length. Whenever you add information to the project documentation, make sure the information goes into the right place, so that all project documents keep their focus.

Discussion   A DOCUMENTATION PORTFOLIO is a first step towards focused information. Such a portfolio describes various types of documents that a project may need, and what their typical contents are. The portfolio takes into account that each document has a distinct group of TARGET READERS. You can fine-tune the focus of any document from the portfolio by adapting it to its intended readers' expectations.

The documents you create in a project form the DOCUMENT LANDSCAPE – a network of related documents that the team members use for communication. The more focused the individual documents are, the clearer the DOCUMENT LANDSCAPE, and as a consequence the more effective it is.

Focused information isn't only desirable for complete documents, but can be broken down to the level of chapters and sections of individual documents. This is true especially for documents that present STRUCTURED INFORMATION – a format that employs stylistic elements to convey the structure of a document and its contents.

Individual Documentation Requirements

Problem   **How can unnecessary documentation requirements be avoided?**

Forces   There are development projects that can do with very little documentation. Small teams working on one site can often do without comprehensive documentation. For example, XP (eXtreme Programming) is well known for producing only a minimum of documentation (Beck 2000).

Other projects, however, require more documentation. Perhaps the project stakeholders ask for more documentation, perhaps the team needs the documents for cross-site communication, perhaps the design needs to be described in more rigour than is possible just using informal discussion.

The cause for differing documentation requirements lies partly in the various methodologies that different teams may follow, and partly in the fact that project scopes differ. We can build new software or we can re-engineer existing systems. Sometimes we design the overall architecture, sometimes we contribute components to a larger whole. A project may involve just one person or hundreds of people.

Moreover, development projects and consultancy projects may attach differing significance to documentation. In development projects, the value of documentation can often be measured by how well the documentation contributes to the communication within the team. In consultancy projects, however, documentation may be the project's goal.

In his book on *Agile Modeling*, Scott Ambler writes: 'Each system has its own unique documentation needs; one size does not fit all', and recommends: 'Keep it just simple enough, but not too simple' (Ambler 2002). In a similar vein, Alistair Cockburn, in his book on *Agile Software Development*, recommends creating documentation that is 'light but sufficient' or 'barely sufficient', and goes on: 'The ideal quantity, "barely sufficient", varies by time and place within any one project.' (Cockburn 2001)

In other words, if you define a standard documentation process for all projects, and force the teams to create all documents that might be useful in any one context, you impose an unnecessary documentation workload on many projects.

Solution   **The most effective approach towards documentation is for each project to define its documentation requirements individually.**

The actual amount of documentation necessary depends on factors like the project's size, whether the team can work on one site or not, and the project's criticality, among other things.

You can break down the 'right' amount of documentation for your project into the following:

- The amount of documentation required by the project stakeholders.

- The amount of documentation the team needs to communicate.

- The amount of documentation individual team members might need to think ideas through.

- The amount of documentation the project will need in a later stage.

- The amount of documentation a follow-up project will probably need.

The individual documentation requirements must define which documents are necessary and what material these documents should cover. Agile documentation encourages you to do without any documents that you consider unnecessary in a concrete situation, but on the other hand, to plan actively for documents that are needed.

Documentation requirements can change over time. More documentation can become necessary, for example towards the end of a project when the team will soon disperse. Or less documentation can become necessary, for example during stages of intense collaboration in which everybody involved can easily communicate directly. Re-evaluating the requirements from time to time is necessary to keep the documentation at the appropriate level of volume and detail.

Discussion   Working out what documentation the team or the project stakeholders need is closely related to working out who the TARGET READERS of potential documents are. The actual task of defining the documentation requirements should be part of any agile project. If you think of documentation as A DISTINCT ACTIVITY, you can define the documentation requirements and the resources you plan to spend in the same way as you plan any other project activity.

Defining the documentation requirements individually for each project does not mean that you have to define them from scratch every time. A DOCUMENT-

ATION PORTFOLIO can show you what documents might be needed and what their contents might be. You can then choose the documents you need and tailor them to your project's specific needs.

Documentation Portfolio

Problem

How can teams reuse the knowledge about which documents might be required in their projects?

Forces

There is no point in defining a standard documentation process, or standard documentation requirements for software projects in general. Software projects are much too diverse for standard requirements to be possible.

Many software projects do however have things in common. For example, almost all software projects make a difference between what a system, a program, or a module does on one hand, and how its internals are designed on the other. This distinction stems from the 'information hiding' principle (Parnas 1972) and it is often reflected in the documentation, resulting in separate documents for the system specification and the system design.

There are other categories of documents that are repeatedly found in project documentation, ranging from documents on testing to documents that explain how to use the software. Many projects require management-oriented documents. Despite the fact that these documents vary greatly in length and detail, there is no reason why every project should re-invent the categories of documents that should be considered when the documentation requirements are defined.

Solution

A documentation portfolio describes which documents might be necessary in a software project, and their scope. If an organisation sets up such a portfolio, projects can choose those documents they need, checking the necessity of each candidate document individually.

A documentation portfolio prevents the team from having to decide which document candidates exist. The portfolio includes a set of suggestions for the team to consider.

Figure 4 presents a documentation portfolio that includes the candidate documents for most software projects. A similar list is given in Scott Ambler's book on *Agile Modeling* in the chapter on documentation (Ambler 2002). You can use this portfolio, or you can tailor it to the typical needs of your organisation's projects.

The documents included in the portfolio fall into the following categories:

- *Management* documents define the management context for a project, such as the overall scope and the project schedule. A typical example is the management summary – a document that describes the overall goals of the project and puts them into a business context. Management documents may also include a short paper that introduces new team members to the project.

- *Specification* documents describe what the software does. This includes aspects as widespread as data, functionality, the user interface, efficiency and more. The primary purpose of specification documents is to clarify exactly what software is needed. Specification documents serve as a basis for discussions with the customer, or as a basis for discussion with teams who work on related tasks. In addition, the specification is what a system can be tested against.

- *Design* documents explain how the software works, including why it works this way. They look at the internals of a system, a module or a class, at its structure and its behaviour. Small overlaps with the specification are possible – the data model, for example, is important during both specification and design. Design documents are used mostly for communication among the development team, but can also be useful for communication with the interested customer. A design document can help pass on the project's expertise to future projects – a knowledge management mechanism that should not be ignored.

- Hardly any project is an island. There is often an old system that is going to be replaced by the new software to some degree, perhaps gradually. This may make a *migration* concept necessary. A migration concept describes how the functionality of the old system gives way to the functionality of the new system, and how the data that was stored by the old system is transformed into data that can be used by the new system.

Project management

- Management summary
- Delivery plan
- Project manual / team guidelines

Requirements specification

- System overview
- Use cases
- Data model
- Functional specification
- User interface specification
- Timed behaviour
- Non-functional requirements (execution speed, maintenance, etc.)
- Glossary

Design

- Architecture overview
- Data model
- Class hierarchy
- Class interaction diagrams
- User interface design / event management
- Database access / transactions
- Integration with neighbouring systems
- Guidelines and naming conventions

Migration

- Functionality migration
- Data migration

Usage

- Usage guidelines / concepts
- Cookbook
- Tutorial

Test

- Use cases
- Test cases
- Test concept

Operations

- Deployment
- Operations guidelines
- Trouble-shooting

Figure 4. A documentation portfolio

- Often tests have to be specified, perhaps using *test* documents. These may overlap with the specification. Use cases, for example, fall into either category (Cockburn 2000). Depending on the actual project and customers' requirements, a complete set of test cases can serve as the system specification, and can make separate specification documents redundant to some degree.

- *Usage* documents describe how a system, module or class can be used. They outline the use of parameters, for example, and the order in which functions can be called, and are often required for system integration. Usage documents may turn out to be no more than a few guidelines, but may amount to an overall usage concept. When you deliver a framework, for example, the usage concept deserves particular attention, as it advises the users how to build a working application.

- *Operations* documents describe how a system is to be operated and how problems with the operation can be tackled.

Many of the documents mentioned above are well known from the literature on software engineering (Sommerville 1996) or from software engineering methods such as the Unified Process (UP) (Jacobsen Booch Rumbaugh 1999, Kruchten 2000).

Your project may or may not need any of the documents listed here, or perhaps you can merge several documents from one category into one document. Perhaps some documents are completely unnecessary in your situation. It is up to the project team to decide what documentation is necessary in a specific situation, taking the customer's requirements into account. A healthy dose of scepticism is fine when it comes to the decision over what project documents should be written. Agile software development encourages us to provide the documentation that is necessary, but to go without unnecessary paperwork.

Discussion   The decision about whether or not a document from the portfolio is needed is closely related to who the TARGET READERS are. If you cannot name the TARGET READERS for a document, the project can probably do without that document. After all, which set of documents you decide to produce depends on the INDIVIDUAL DOCUMENTATION REQUIREMENTS of your project. A UP project is likely to come to different conclusions than an XP project.

Documents from the portfolio can vary in scope and level of detail. A FOCUS ON LONG-TERM RELEVANCE helps you to include information that is useful in the long term and to produce documents with high significance. On the other hand, information that will soon be irrelevant probably doesn't need to be documented.

Overview documents typically attract the highest number of readers. Management summaries, architecture overviews and so on describe THE BIG PICTURE of a project or a system. To many projects, these documents are among the most important ones within the portfolio.

More detailed documents, however, are in the centre of the trade-off between verbal and written communication. A specification document, for example, is typically the result of a requirement analysis. It can complement discussions with the customer, but it can never replace these discussions. (See also SPECIFICATION AS A JOINT EFFORT.) Almost all projects need a specification document, but not necessarily one at the finest possible level of detail.

Similarly, design documentation is necessary and useful in most projects. In most cases, however, design documents need not be concerned with low-level technical details, which are better communicated face-to-face. Design documents should instead focus on the DESIGN RATIONALE – the motivation that led to the design decisions the team has made.

Finally, the classification given by the documentation portfolio contributes to the goal of presenting FOCUSED INFORMATION. It roughly sketches which documents you might need and outlines how these documents can focus on a particular topic.

Focus on Long-Term Relevance

Problem   **How can projects avoid producing documentation that expires too soon?**

Forces   Software project documentation deals with a most diverse set of information. The information you rely on ranges from specification to design, from overall principles to technical details, from team-oriented to customer-oriented.

In an agile project, we don't automatically document all this information in writing. An agile project avoids spending more resources on documentation than necessary, and concentrates on those documents that have a clear purpose that justifies the time and effort that go into their production.

Moreover, if you decided to prepare documents for each aspect of the project, you might choose written communication as a medium indiscriminately and without regard for its appropriateness.

These factors lead to the question: how can you determine whether a written document is appropriate or not?

Let's take a look at a software project done in an agile fashion. People exchange ideas frequently through discussions and informal communication. Much of the information that is exchanged is important on the spur of the moment, to help team members make progress with their current work. Not all this information will be relevant a couple of months or years later.

Some will, however. Being agile doesn't mean being short-sighted. The literature on agile development reminds us that while delivering the software is the primary goal of a development project, preparing for future projects is a secondary goal that should not be ignored (Ambler 2002). This is what Alistair Cockburn means by 'preparing for the next game' (Cockburn 2001). To prepare for a later project stage, or for a future project, you have to capture the knowledge that others will rely on.

This is the point where documentation can unfold its greatest benefit: knowledge that must be preserved for the future is worth documenting.

This isn't a mere assumption. Knowledge preservation has been the subject of much discussion and much research. For example, Stuart Brand emphasises the importance of digital and non-digital libraries in his book on long-term thinking and planning, *The Clock of the Long Now* (Brand 1999).

Solution   **There is much value in documentation that focuses on issues with a long-term relevance – issues that will play a role in a later project phase or in future projects.**

Documentation is essentially an instrument for knowledge management, both within a project and across projects:

- Documents, when they describe the fundamentals of a project, are important throughout all projects phases. Examples include an essential specification, or a central document that describes the software architecture. The long-term relevance of these issues suggests that they should be captured in written form.

- The lessons learned from a project are often useful for future projects. Insight gained into the software architecture, design decisions or conclusions drawn at a project retrospective are all candidates for written documentation.

There is less value in the comprehensive documentation of things with only short-term relevance. If, due to limited resources, not everything can be documented – which is almost always the case – preference should be given to topics with long-term significance.

Discussion This pattern is closely related to the TARGET READERS pattern. Both patterns raise the issue of whether producing a document is justified or not. Raising this question is essential when you choose the documents that your project needs from the DOCUMENTATION PORTFOLIO. Several examples exist of documents that are typically characterised by a long-term relevance and are almost always justified: a document that describes THE BIG PICTURE, a specification document, provided the team performed the SPECIFICATION AS A JOINT EFFORT with the customer, and a document for the DESIGN RATIONALE.

If a topic has long-term relevance and needs to be documented beyond the limits of the current project, long-term availability becomes an issue. To have the TARGET READERS benefit from the document, it must be widely available. This is essentially a matter of documentation management, and is addressed in the INFORMATION MARKETPLACE and KNOWLEDGE MANAGEMENT patterns.

Specification as a Joint Effort

Problem **How can development projects ensure that they head in the direction the customer wants?**

Forces The specification of a software system requires a lot of input from domain experts. A close collaboration between the software experts and the domain experts is necessary to make sure that the software meets the customer's expectations. The project team must learn from the domain experts what the software is supposed to do. This collaboration involves a lot of face-to-face communication.

However, it is dangerous to rely on verbal communication alone, for two reasons. First, there can be misunderstanding between the project team and the customer that even a series of thorough discussions won't reveal. Often, you may think you have reached a common understanding during a discussion, but when you try to commit your understanding to paper, you find this isn't the case. A written specification is much less likely to let misunderstandings go unnoticed.

Second, a written document can avoid quarrels over who is right and who is wrong, should differing opinions arise over the system requirements, perhaps several months into the project. Even the friendliest customer relationship suffers when accusations are made that the team designed the wrong software. A written specification largely avoids such accusations.

This is even more true when more than two parties are involved. This is not uncommon – often several software companies collaborate on a project, and different departments of the customer's organisation may also have a stake in the project. In such a project a written specification gives all parties some planning safety.

This does not mean that the system has to be specified down to the finest detail, nor does it mean that the requirements cannot undergo change. It is acceptable to leave details open in the specification, but the specification must make this clear, so that the team is aware of decisions that still have to be made.

Changing requirements are considered natural in an agile project that follows an iterative development process. The specification document helps to deal with changing requirements in an acceptable manner, updating the project plan and perhaps re-scheduling deadlines accordingly.

Solution   **Every development project requires a specification, which reflects the requirement analysis done jointly by the project team and the customer.**

Writing the specification should be much like keeping a record of what has been said during the discussion of the requirements. Nowhere is it as important as here that face-to-face communication and documentation complement each other:

* The specification document describes the common understanding of the system that the project team and the customer have achieved, and provides the team with the information necessary to begin the design.

- Use cases, stories and scenarios provided by the domain experts usually furnish excellent input for the specification document. Sometimes a sufficiently complete set of use cases can be all the specification document requires, as long as the use cases are sufficiently detailed to ensure that the project team and the customer have reached a common understanding.

- The specification document can be used to get further discussions started. You can take an initial specification document to the domain experts for feedback, so improving the specification.

It is important that all stakeholders agree on this specification. This requires more than a general agreement from whoever represents the customer's organisation as a whole. Stakeholder agreement requires a common understanding shared by the team and all departments of the customer's organisation, in fact by all individuals involved.

Discussion   As much as this pattern stresses that a close collaboration with the customer is necessary for producing a good specification, you shouldn't draw the conclusion that other documents won't require similar collaboration. In fact all project documents do. The point here, and the motivation for this particular pattern, is that the requirements specification deserves an especially close collaboration between the project team and the customer from day one.

This principle has much been stressed in the literature on agile development. The Agile Manifesto (in one of its follow-up recommendations) suggests that 'business people and developers work together daily throughout the project', as cited in Alistair Cockburn's book (Cockburn 2001). Alistair Cockburn comments: '...the longer it takes to get information to and from the developers, the more damage will occur to the project'. Scott Ambler cites active stakeholder participation as one of the core principles of *Agile Modeling* (Ambler 2002).

The role of customer collaboration has also been the subject of many other works. For example, Jim Coplien, in his organisational patterns, recommends that you *Engage Customers* (Coplien 1995) not only in quality assurance, but also in specification and design.

Still, customer collaboration can be hard, as it requires you to speak a common language. One way to ease this problem is to plan for a CUSTOMER REVIEW.

In addition, speaking a common language is more difficult in the abstract than in the concrete. Customer collaboration can profit a lot from working on REALISTIC EXAMPLES to which both the project team and the customer can easily relate. This is, among other things, why use cases are so particularly useful.

Design Rationale

Problem

How can the team make sure that the foundations are laid for future design changes?

Forces

Most projects choose to document the design of the system they're building. A design document describes the system's interfaces as well as its internal functioning, typically addressing both structural and behavioural aspects. The purpose of such a document is to convey the system design to other team members, to customers or to future projects.

Such a design description is fair enough, as it can prove useful during system maintenance.

When a system undergoes change, however, a mere account of the actual design might not be sufficient. As the design evolves, it is important that the team is aware of why the design was chosen in the first place and what other design options might exist. However, implementation details are likely to change whenever the software changes, so won't be of much long-term use.

Solution

Design documents become a valuable source of information if they aren't restricted to describing the actual design, but also focus on the rationale behind the design and explain why the particular design was chosen.

The more experience a design document reveals, the more useful it can be for future projects. It is the lessons learned from the system design that makes a design document a valuable contribution to the project documentation.

This leads to the following guidelines:

- The design document should not only be concerned with the results of the design process, but should explain the reasons that led to the actual design.

- The design document should explore possible design alternatives, discuss their pros and cons, and explain why these alternatives were declined.

The rationale behind a design is what is useful for team members who need to understand the internals of the software, perhaps because they have to maintain, extend or improve it, perhaps because they would like to re-use the concept, at least partially, on their project, or otherwise profit from the experiences made.

On the other hand, good design documents can often do without technical details of the actual coding.

Discussion   This pattern is very much in sync with the desire to put a FOCUS ON LONG-TERM RELEVANCE. Specific design details may be of little interest after a while, and therefore might not require documentation. The overall design will still be essential years after the system was first launched, however, and is therefore a good candidate for documentation, along with the reasons that led to the design.

The explanation of the design rationale can gain significantly from the use of REALISTIC EXAMPLES. Use cases, or other scenarios, help explain the principles behind the design that was chosen, as well as its pros and cons.

The Big Picture

Problem   **How can people be introduced to a project without being confronted with a deluge of technical details?**

Forces   When people look at a painting in a gallery, they often step back and look from a short distance. This allows them to see the painting as a whole. If they stood right in front of it, they would be able to see the detail, but the overall impression would be lost.

By analogy, project documentation sometimes deals with many technical details – specification details, design details and the like. These details may be crucial to a successful project, and documenting them can be useful. However, it is sometimes hard to see the wood for the trees.

In *The Mythical Man Month*, Frederick Brooks explains: 'Most documentation fails in giving too little overview. The trees are described, the bark and leaves are commented, but there is no map of the forest.' (Brooks 1995)

Detailed material, as useful as it may be for people who are already experts, isn't much help for those new to a topic, who would like to understand a concept, or who need to get an introduction into new material.

However, the documentation must also cater for people who aren't yet experts but who are going to familiarise themselves with the project. Think of people who join a team, or think of customers who will maintain a system once it has been completed. Such people need to get a feel for the project before they can even start to work on the details.

Solution   **A good feel for a project is best conveyed through a description of the 'big picture' of the architecture that underlies the system under construction.**

A big picture document can provide some overall understanding:

- The big picture describes the overall architecture, shows how the entire system is composed of subsystems and modules, and explains the basics of the system's dynamic behaviour.

- The big picture explains the design principles and motivates the decisions that led to the actual design.

- The big picture names the technology that is fundamental to building the system.

- The big picture intentionally abstracts over any details, technical or otherwise, that are irrelevant to an overview.

Preferably, a big picture document should be fairly short and concise – a lengthy document couldn't provide the brief introduction that most readers need, and would probably turn out to be counter-intuitive. For the vast majority of projects, 10 or at most 20 pages are enough. The big picture document can provide links to other, more detailed documents whenever necessary, as Figure 5 illustrates.

Beyond providing an overall understanding, a big picture document is perfectly suited to get discussions started. Mainly because a big picture is of general interest, but also because it's typically short, a big picture document easily finds readers. If you need to have a discussion with the team or with the customer on any issues concerning the overall system architecture, pass the description of the big picture around and you have a perfect starting point.

Discussion   This pattern shows how you can provide an overview without losing yourself in technical detail. Despite the desire for brevity, a big picture document often profits from the inclusion of REALISTIC EXAMPLES, as such examples will

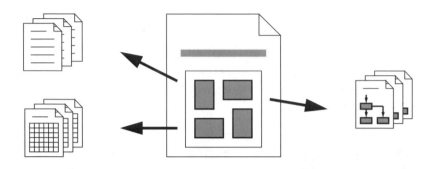

Figure 5. A big picture document providing pointers to the details

help the readers get a feel for the architecture. You can certainly add value to the big picture document if you take the word *picture* seriously and provide JUDICIOUS DIAGRAMS that help you argue your case.

All documentation can profit from a REVIEW CULTURE that provides authors with valuable feedback. A document that presents the big picture can benefit especially from a review that takes A DISTANT VIEW, and so focuses on the overall impression rather than on details.

Separation of Description and Evaluation

Problem   **How can authors prevent loss of credibility?**

Forces   In development projects, much of the project documentation deals with analysis, design, architecture, tests and the like. The nature of these documents is to a large extent descriptive.

However, sometimes you are required to draw a conclusion, make an evaluation, or even come up with your personal opinion. Perhaps you, as a skilled and experienced software engineer, are asked for your opinion on a certain design or a certain concept. A strategy paper, for example, typically includes personal views and concludes with the recommendation of one specific concept or strategy.

Personal views are even more common in documents that emerge from consultancy projects. If you work on a consultancy project it may be the central part of your job to come up with an assessment or a recommendation. We can see that both descriptive material and personal opinions can be necessary and useful.

But while both are necessary and useful, they're not the same thing. It's important to tell them apart.

For an analogy, let's take a brief look at the realm of journalism. It is a good rule of thumb that you should make it clear whether an article in a newspaper or a journal presents facts, or whether it expresses the author's opinion (Glasser 1992). We can adopt this rule of thumb for our purposes. It isn't good style to try to influence readers by confusing description and judgement – readers might doubt the contents of a document that seems to be suggestive.

Solution   **Authors gain credibility if, in their documents, they clearly separate description from evaluation.**

The following table shows roughly how different kinds of information can be classified:

Description	Evaluation
Facts	Judgement
Observations	Author's opinions
Analysis	Recommendation
Data	Validation
Statistics	Interpretation

The separation of description and evaluation must be clear to readers. There are various ways to achieve this goal:

- The separation of description and evaluation can be reflected in the document's structure. You can reserve certain sections of a document for analysis, and draw conclusions or come up with a recommendation in a separate section.

- You can use layout techniques, such as special boxes, extra columns, or type variations to make clear to the readers that certain material isn't a fully objective description, but represents your opinion or the conclusions that you draw.

In addition, you can draw on your command of the language to support the separation of description and evaluation. Descriptive material should not implicitly include any judgement: adjectives such as *good*, *desirable*, *reasonable*, *useful* or *bad*, *problematic*, etc. must be used carefully when describing facts or observations.

Discussion   The separation of description and evaluation contributes to the general goal of presenting FOCUSED INFORMATION. Material presented in a document, or in a section, is supposed to have a clear focus. One precondition for a clear focus is not to confuse description and evaluation.

Using layout techniques to support the separation of description and evaluation is particularly useful when you choose to organise documents as STRUCTURED INFORMATION. You can then employ structural elements, such as textual blocks or cells within UNAMBIGUOUS TABLES, to visualise the separation of description and evaluation. Similarly, the CAREFUL USE OF TYPE VARIATIONS can make that separation clearly visible.

Realistic Examples

Problem   **How can abstract material be explained in a comprehensible way?**

Forces   Most people work better from the concrete to the abstract than vice versa. Technical material, however, is sometimes abstract and difficult to understand. Furthermore, not all readers of a project document are necessarily experts in the field. Material is usually more successfully presented when it is accompanied by convincing examples.

Moreover, readers are sometimes sceptical when a document gives only general advice. Examples can provide evidence that what is said in a document is substantial information.

However, 'toy' examples can have the opposite effect on readers. When a major point is explained only with a toy example, readers are led to believe that the point is not substantial, and that a suggested solution might not work in practical cases.

On the other hand, huge examples or a large number of extensive examples can break the flow of a document and can increase its volume unnecessarily. Including more example material than necessary isn't desirable, either.

Solution   **Project documents are much more convincing if they include realistic examples from the project's context.**

Discussions among the team or with the customers will normally reveal many appropriate examples:

- When you specify the software with your customer you'll normally develop use cases and scenarios. These use cases and scenarios represent valuable input to a specification document. In some projects they can make up the entire specification.

- When you explain a technical design or the system architecture, it is still a good idea to rely on examples from typical use cases. This makes your explanation easier to follow and demonstrates that your design tackles the right problems.

- Consultancy projects aren't necessarily concerned with a concrete development task and may not have concrete use cases to rely on. Realistic examples are still useful, such as typical scenarios from the problem domain.

When realistic examples are too large to be presented in their entirety, it is acceptable to use only an extract or to ignore irrelevant details. It is important that the examples are taken from real-world material, though.

Discussion   This pattern applies to almost all documents from the DOCUMENTATION PORTFOLIO. When you carry out the SPECIFICATION AS A JOINT EFFORT with the customer, you can learn from use cases and scenarios, and you can include them in your documents as well. When you prepare a design document, you can illustrate the DESIGN RATIONALE with examples that demonstrate the pros and cons of any design alternatives the project may have.

When choosing examples, you have to keep in mind who the TARGET READERS for your document are. You have to tailor the examples to the intended readers' backgrounds and expectations, so that they can understand the examples and the examples prove as helpful as they are intended to.

Experience Reports

In the following I'd like to present some experience reports that show how the patterns of this chapter were applied in several real-world projects. I'll refer to several projects from the list at the beginning of this book.

Individual Requirements The first thing that springs to mind is how different the requirements for documentation were in these projects. On one hand, take a development project such as Paracelsus. The team was small and the collaboration with the customer quite close. Everybody knew what they were doing from the start, and having only little documentation was no problem. The documents produced were lightweight, in a positive sense.

Project Paracelsus: minimum documentation

In this small project the task was clear from the start: the customer needed certain components for data transformation that they were going to integrate into a framework they were building. Close collaboration came naturally. The team and the customer decided early on that a minimum amount of documentation would be sufficient.

The specification that was produced consisted essentially of the notes that someone had taken during a small workshop in which the customer explained what the components were supposed to do.

Simultaneously with design and coding, the team produced a design paper and a usage concept. The design paper documented the basic ideas behind the data transformation components. The paper was made available to the customer as input for a second workshop, in which the team and the customer checked that the components' design and the overall framework design were compatible, before coding began. The usage concept provided information about how the components could be called, which parameters had to be supplied and so on. The customer used this concept a lot when they integrated the components into their framework.

Consider Project AirView. The specification document focused on the definition of use cases. As the team had chosen to build a prototype, a lengthy specification of the user interface geometry became unnecessary. The team had understood that discussing the user interface using the prototype was much more effective than producing endless specifications. The amount of documentation could therefore be reduced significantly.

Project AirView: GUI specification

The project's goal was to develop a new graphical user interface, so an important task was to specify what that interface should look like. Nevertheless, the project team and the customer agreed that the specification document should not include a fully-fledged description of the user interface geometry. The specification document defined the use cases the interface would implement, but intentionally left out details of the visual appearance.

The specification of the use cases turned out to be quite important. It was done jointly by the project team and the customer, and the process of committing the use cases to paper clarified many details.

To describe the user interface geometry, the team instead chose to build a prototype. This prototype acted as a living specification. It was given to the customer for reviews, it could be adapted quickly, and it provided much input, both more quickly and more concretely than an abstract specification could have done.

On the other hand, some projects did require a more comprehensive documentation.

Project FlexiCar (see page 48), for instance, required more comprehensive documentation because many people were involved, and because it was clear from the start that system maintenance would eventually be handed over from the project team to the customer.

Next, there is Project Extricate (see page 48). This project was a huge re-engineering effort. A specification of what the new system should look like was not enough. The team always had to keep the migration from the old system to the new system in mind. This migration was crucial for the project's success, and it was necessary to document it, so that the many stakeholders could examine it.

Project Persistor was a large effort, involving many people from different teams and different companies. Because the goal of this project was to develop a framework, more documents from the DOCUMENTATION PORTFOLIO became

Project FlexiCar: detailed design description

When the project started, the customer already had a clear idea of how their car manufacturing process could be improved and accelerated. The project team was still small at the time, and it produced an overview document that summarised the customer's requirements. The document also sketched the architecture the team had in mind. The customer reviewed the document, ensuring that the team was heading in the right direction.

The lead designer then set up a document that described the system architecture in more detail, refining this document as the project progressed. This document was quite technical, as it was intended mainly for software engineers. The document served two purposes. First, it was used to communicate the principles behind the architecture to the entire team. At some point, the project involved up to 50 people, so couldn't rely on verbal communication alone. The design document clearly facilitated knowledge exchange. Second, the document was later to be used by team members from the customer, who were to maintain the system beyond the project's time frame.

Project Extricate: mapping from old to new

This project faced two major challenges. First, it involved many people: the project team, software engineers from the customer, and domain experts from the customer. Each of these parties had contributions to make, and each had to have their say. Second, as this was a re-engineering project, the team first had to familiarise themselves with the old system and its application domain.

The functional specification was easy: the system's functionality wasn't going to be changed at all. The system had to be refactored to become more flexible though. The team had to search the system for hard-coded properties of life insurance products, and had to understand what these properties meant so that they could accurately be extracted into a database. This involved several subtle and intricate details, which easily went unnoticed during discussions with the customer. Often the domain experts took things for granted that the software engineers hadn't even thought of.

A specification document was a great help as far as detecting such misunderstandings was concerned. The specification represented what the team had understood of the various insurance products, and was given to the domain experts for review. The domain experts used the specification to verify the mapping from the old, hard-coded properties to the new properties. The discussions spawned by this document revealed many important details. The document was updated several times following the discussion, and served as a reliable source of information.

One other document was particularly important: the migration strategy paper. First, it revealed the dependencies between the migration of different subsystems – which subsystems had to be migrated before others and so on. Second, the migration paper demonstrated that there was a trade-off between the quality of the new data model and the complexity of the migration process: the better the new data model was, the more complex the mapping from old to new would become. On the other hand, the simpler the migration was kept, the more flaws would be carried from the old data model to the new one. The customer appreciated this discussion a lot.

necessary. First of all, this included a usage concept. The framework users had to learn how to incorporate the framework into their applications: as they worked on different sites, documentation was indispensable. Second, the framework documentation included a design concept that was needed for future maintenance and refactoring (see page 50).

These experience reports clearly demonstrate that the projects did have INDIVIDUAL DOCUMENTATION REQUIREMENTS. Some projects were fine with a minimum of documentation, while others would have been in serious trouble without more comprehensive documentation. The key idea of agile documentation is not to go without comprehensive documentation in each and every project, but to make sure that all documents are justified by the benefit they represent for the TARGET READERS.

Despite the varying documentation requirements, there are several things that, in my experience, all successful projects have in common, as far as documentation is concerned. When I reviewed the projects to find out about what kind of documentation worked and what didn't, I noticed some things over and over again.

The Need for a Specification

First, no project can do without a specification, and agile projects are no exception. Almost all of the development projects I looked at produced specification documents, and those that didn't regretted this strategy. The experience reports from Projects FlexiCar, Extricate and Persistor show that they all produced a specification (or received one from the customer), and they all made good use of it.

Of all the specification documents I have seen, some were rather short, some were more detailed. In most cases, a less detailed specification was no disadvantage, because many specification details only evolved over time. Projects Paracelsus and AirView demonstrate that it is more crucial to success to regard

Project Persistor: documenting a framework

Documentation played an important role, as this project involved many people from many companies, even in different cities, and because the contributions from the different parties had to be integrated closely. The team tried to keep the documentation within reasonable proportions, mostly with success, though also with a few problems.

After the project's kick-off, the team produced an initial specification of the data access layer framework. The specification was quite short, won the customer's approval, and was used as the basis for design. However, as the project evolved, additional requirements came to light, some of which were implemented, others not. In the heat of the project, however, these additional requirements were never specified in writing. After a while this led to conflicting views about which additional functions had to be implemented and which had been declined. At this point the relationship between the customer, the framework developers and the other projects became rather tense. The main problem wasn't that there were conflicting views, but that the conflict hadn't been resolved properly when it had first arisen. All parties felt that specifying the additional requirements in writing would have been useful, not to introduce bureaucracy into the project, but to increase the awareness of what changes were necessary, who was in charge, and the consequences on schedules.

The most important problem the project faced was how to train the other teams to integrate the framework into their applications. As teams from different cities were involved, face-to-face communication alone was insufficient. The team decided to use a mix of documentation and workshops. A usage concept for the framework was passed to all other teams. This document explained how the framework could be configured for use by a concrete application, how its interface methods could be called, and the general guidelines to be followed. Once the teams had familiarised themselves with the ideas behind the framework and the use guidelines, the framework team ran workshops in which they explained in detail how to adapt the framework to individual project's needs. These workshops took from several days to several weeks, complementing the understanding that the usage concept had supplied.

Although testing played a huge role, the team, along with the customer, decided that documenting the test cases was unnecessary. Instead, the team implemented a large number of test cases, and extended and maintained the test code as the project progressed. As the tests were executable, they served the project much better than any test document could have done.

Project Navigator: confusion due to a lack of specification

This team had to develop several user interface elements that were rather complex in their appearance and their behaviour. The time frame was fairly short and the deadlines were tight. Software development had to be fast, and lightweight documents were a must.

The project team and the customer had agreed on the following documents for each user interface component: a brief specification describing appearance and behaviour, a design document consisting of a UML diagram and an interface description, and a document on test cases.

There had to be agreement on the specification, not only among the team and the customer, but also with the customer's customer – the car manufacturer that would ultimately buy the navigation system. Unfortunately, the ultimate customer was consistently late in committing themselves to a particular GUI specification, but urged the team to begin with the design and the implementation nevertheless. At some point, the team was asked to begin the coding, although component specifications weren't available. Code was written – but later had to be re-written completely.

In retrospect, the team felt that the project would have profited if it hadn't tried to do without a written specification. A specification document could have clarified which parts of the specification were settled and which were still open. The design and implementation could have focused on those parts that were clear, leaving room for changes in the hot spots. Without any specification, the team felt they weren't getting anywhere near the desired result, and morale was low.

Otherwise the lightweight documentation worked well. The design documents and the test documents consisted of only a few pages each, but contained all information necessary for the customer to integrate the components.

the SPECIFICATION AS A JOINT EFFORT than to complete the specification to the smallest detail. In other words, an incomplete specification may be fine, as long it is clear that it is incomplete, and as long it is clear which parts are still to be decided.

In a few cases, however, a project did not have a specification at all. At one stage Project Navigator suffered this fate. No written specification was available until well into the project: a few informal statements were all the team could rely on when they were asked to begin coding. In the end, much code had to be deleted and re-written. As a consequence, morale among the team was low.

Project Persistor did produce a specification, but failed to maintain it over the course of the project, and in particular, over the course of several change requests. As a consequence, misunderstandings over the specification became an increasing nuisance. Better maintenance of the specification would have made things easier for all parties involved.

Overviews   A second observation I have made is that no project can go without THE BIG PICTURE. Whatever may be the necessary level of detail for the documentation of your project, you always need an overview of the system you're building.

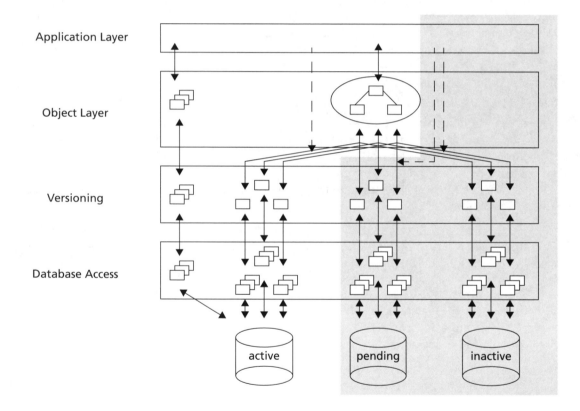

Figure 6. Project Persistor: the big picture of the multi-layered framework architecture

Project Persistor provides a good example. In this project the team produced a specification, a design concept, a usage concept and test cases. Apart from the usage concept, which was heavily used by the framework users, the information that received most attention was the framework's 'big picture' that was presented within the design document. The big picture was essentially a diagram that showed the multi-tier architecture, demonstrated the database access and explained the different object states. It is shown in Figure 6. The team used this diagram a lot when they defined the framework's architecture, and used it to communicate the architecture to the other teams.

Project Vista also relied on a big picture document a lot – actually this project *lived* on THE BIG PICTURE. The big picture here was a diagram that outlined the organisation's application landscape, as shown in Figure 7. The diagram itself doesn't contain much detail. For example, the interfaces between the systems aren't properly specified. Yet this diagram was used in so many discussions and conjured up so many good ideas that the project would not have been the same without it.

Project Vista: discussing the application landscape

Analysing the application landscape involved talking to many people, as well as browsing through existing documentation. It turned out that some of the system interfaces were documented in detail, while others weren't documented at all. However, the main problem was that nobody knew exactly what relationships existed between the systems. It was even difficult to get a complete list of all systems involved. An overview was much missed.

One of the main results of this project was the overview diagram of the application landscape given in Figure 7, in which boxes represent the systems and arrows represent the various kinds of relationships between these systems. This big picture diagram was used many times to get a discussion started. It got the customer 'hooked' immediately. Many people looked at it, made additions and corrections, and so provided a lot of valuable insight. The diagram was updated several times during the project with every step forward the system analysis made.

An entirely different document was devoted to the technological risks that the project had identified. The risks were judged with respect to their relevance as well as their probability.

Project Webber (see page 56) is yet another example of how important THE BIG PICTURE can be. The goal of this fairly small project was to set up a Web site, and the customer was much concerned with the design of the site map.

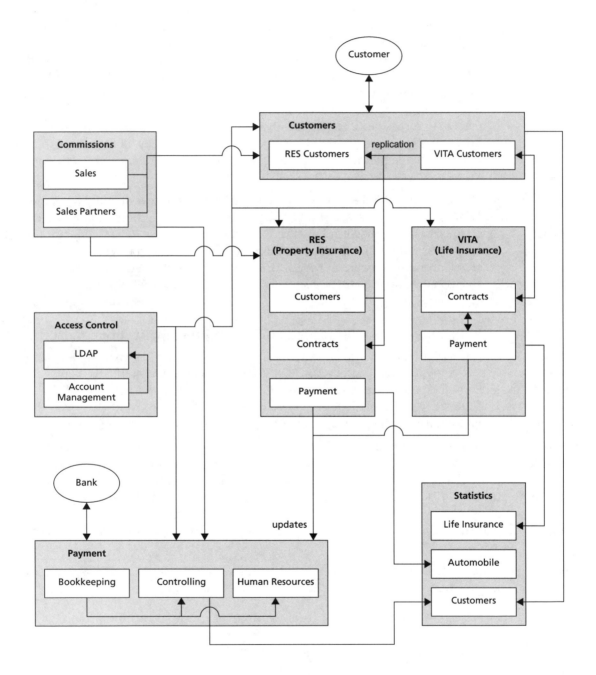

Figure 7. Project Vista: the application landscape

As a consequence, the diagram that gave an overview of the site map became the most important document (Figure 8).

Project OpenDoors shows the problems that arise from not having a 'big picture' document. In this project the team produced quite comprehensive documentation on the portal they developed, some of which was useful and some of which wasn't. As there was no document that described the portal's overall architecture, obtaining an overview was difficult, and inconsistent views of the overall architecture emerged.

Project OpenDoors: communicating the design

As this project involved several teams, a certain degree of documentation was necessary to manage the communication between these teams. Nevertheless, little documentation was produced for the specification of the web portal. The reason was that the specification was done when the team was still small, and that people from both the software company and the customer were on that team.

When it came to implementing the design, however, more people were involved and documentation of the design became necessary. Unfortunately this led to a number of overlapping design documents, which, at least in places, offered conflicting views. The project documentation was rather confusing at this point. The individual teams had provided design documents that described the individual subsystems, but there was no description of the overall architecture that would hold all parts together. Moreover, the design documents included a number of details that would soon be outdated due to changed requirements.

The documentation mirrored the actual design. The individual designs of the subsystems had gone separate ways, and after a while it became difficult to integrate them into a common architecture. At that point the project decided to consolidate the architecture. This was accompanied by writing an architecture document that explained how the different subsystems were to collaborate to form a web portal. This document referenced some of the earlier design documents for details, but profited a lot from the fact that it could do without fast-changing details itself.

These examples not only show that big picture documents are important, they also demonstrate *why* big picture documents are so important. Big picture documents often build a bridge between written documentation and face-to-face communication. They attract the readers' attention and invite them to ask team members for more detailed information.

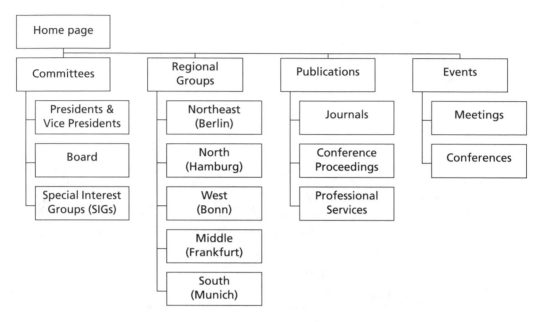

Figure 8. Project Webber: the site map

Project Webber: a long-lived diagram

At project kick-off the team and the customer met in a small workshop session to discuss the contents and the structure of the Web site. It turned out that the site map was supposed to mirror the hierarchical structure of the customer's organisation. As a result the team provided a diagram that gave an overview of the intended structure (Figure 8). This diagram became the central part of the specification. This intentionally ignored details such as the layout of the individual web pages or the full list of hyperlinks that had to be included, as these details would change frequently. In addition, only a small concept paper was produced that described how to configure the web server and how to integrate content into the Web site.

The diagram served its purpose well. It was used throughout several discussions. After the consultancy project finished the customer still used this diagram for the further development of their Web site.

Projects Persistor, Vista and Webber give powerful evidence of the fact that written documentation and face-to-face communication aren't opposed to each other. The same phenomenon can be observed in other projects as well.

Credibility

My third observation is that the SEPARATION OF DESCRIPTION AND EVALUATION does a lot of good, although many people aren't very aware of this principle. Project Vista, for example, described the application landscape and the architectural risks separately. Project Contentis made a clear separation between the requirements and the actual recommendation of a tool. Both projects gained credibility in this way.

Project Contentis: requirements and recommendation

The team began with an analysis of how the customer would like to use a content management system. The team interviewed the customer, the customer responded, the team pinned down what they had understood, and the customer reviewed what had been written. What emerged was a sufficiently accurate understanding of the future processes. From this understanding the team derived a list of requirements for the content management system.

Next, the team contacted several vendors and asked them to run workshops in which they should demonstrate how their systems worked. They were given the requirements document so they could prepare for the workshops. They were also given a description of a concrete use case – the web newsletter the customer wanted to implement. In the workshops the vendors demonstrated how the newsletter could be implemented with their systems, and to which degree their systems fulfilled the requirements.

The team concluded the project with an evaluation document that mirrored how the team felt the different products on the market matched the requirements. The team provided both: a requirements document, clearly objective, following a thorough analysis, and an evaluation document, influenced by the impressions from the workshops.

It was clear that the recommendation made in the evaluation document included personal views. Ultimately, it was the customer who decided which system they were going to use.

Preserving the Knowledge

Finally, I'd like to stress once more the importance of keeping a FOCUS ON LONG-TERM RELEVANCE. During the review of many projects I noticed the importance of documents that describe things that matter in the long term, especially the DESIGN RATIONALE. Two projects demonstrate this importance particularly well.

In the case of Project Persistor, the DESIGN RATIONALE was exactly what was missing from the design concept. The consequence was that the design concept turned out to be less useful as it could have been, and the team experienced significant trouble during the framework's maintenance that could have been avoided.

Project FlexiCar was more successful at capturing the DESIGN RATIONALE. The design document outlined why the particular design had been chosen, named the pros and cons of several design alternatives, and used REALISTIC EXAMPLES to explain these decisions. This was a precondition for the software's longevity, and contributed much to the project's success.

Project Persistor: difficulties with changed requirements

Two years after the first release of the data access layer framework, the implementation of the object versioning mechanism had to be changed due to new requirements, and in order to increase the framework's time performance. Only a few people from the original team were still on the project, and they weren't familiar with the pros and cons of the various design alternatives the team had evaluated two years previously.

This was the moment when the design concept was consulted. Unfortunately, it gave little information on the motivation behind the actual design. It did describe the principles of the design that had been chosen, but it didn't mention the reasons, nor why any alternative designs had been rejected. A good degree of reverse engineering became necessary to work out what alternatives existed and what the various trade-offs were. Had the rationale behind the original design been documented, the team would have been able to react to the new requirements much more quickly.

Project FlexiCar: managing the design responsibility

The lead architect had produced a design document that, over the years, was heavily used. First, it represented an ideal starting point for new team members to learn about the system's architecture. The document didn't just describe the system, but also explained the motivation for the design decisions. For example, the document explained *why* an application server was used and *why* bean-managed persistence had been given preference over container-managed persistence with the EJBs (Enterprise Java Beans), and so on.

Second, when the project reached its end, the team was reduced and software engineers from the customer were to maintain the system. These software engineers had been on the project, so they already knew a lot about the architecture, although they hadn't invented it. The design document, however, allowed them to understand the motivation behind design decisions made one or two years before. The fact that such a design document was available made it easier for them to accept responsibility for system maintenance and possible future extensions.

2 Structuring Individual Documents

Voluminous documentation is part of the problem, not part of the solution.

Tom DeMarco, Timothy Lister (DeMarco Lister 1987)

Have you ever looked for something in a document and been unable to find it, even though you knew you had the right document? You probably have – this problem is common enough.

In most cases, voluminous documentation isn't exactly a service to readers. Despite the intention to provide readers with comprehensive information, voluminous documentation often veils knowledge when it should instead convey it.

Unfortunately, project documents are sometimes quite lengthy and poorly organised. If readers are faced with such documents, it may be ages before they find the information they're looking for.

At some point they just give up. Frustrated with going through a document over and over again, they resort to other ways of obtaining the same information, or decide to try to get by without it.

This is the moment at which a document has ultimately failed to serve its purpose. Such a document is a waste of time, both for those who wrote it and for those who must read it.

Before I present the patterns that address this problem, let's do a little experiment. I'd like to ask you to look at the excerpts from project documents given in Figure 9 and Figure 10, to see which you prefer.

Deployment Processes for Web Content

There are essentially two different ways to deploy content to the web: one for editorial changes, and the other for structural changes. Editorial changes are made by editors and are hot-deployed to the web. Structural changes influence the content's programming, such as Java code within JSPs, and undergo testing before they are released.

Web content is stored and edited in a content management system (CMS). In the following, we explain in more detail how the two deployment processes from the CMS to the web look like.

To make editorial changes, an editor adds or updates content in the CMS. Once this is done, an editor-in-chief reviews and publishes the content. Publishing means that the editor-in-chief calls a function offered by the CMS, which results in the new or modified content being deployed directly to the web server. The web server need not be restarted.

Structural changes are performed by a programmer who makes changes to the JSP programming within the templates used in the CMS. Once these changes are finished, the programmer calls a function that exports the content from the CMS into a file system structure known as the transfer area. Next, the programmer invokes a process that transfers the contents onto a test server. The programmer then tests the changes with a web server that runs on the test machine. Programming and testing are repeated until the tests are successful. The changes are now ready to be published to the web. To do this, a web server administrator stops the web server process, transfers the modified content from the test machine to the web server, and re-starts the web server process.

Figure 9. Excerpt from a project document

These two documents look quite different, although they contain the same information. Their appearance and structure couldn't be more different, though. The first excerpt consists of a few paragraphs, while the second features stronger structural elements and a diagram for illustration.

Interestingly, the second excerpt is longer than the first one. But it isn't as dense, and due to its improved structure has less of a voluminous feel.

Deployment Processes for Web Content

There are essentially two different ways to deploy content to the web: one for editorial changes, and the other for structural changes. Editorial changes are made by editors and are hot-deployed to the web. Structural changes influence the content's programming, such as Java code within JSPs, and undergo testing before they are released.

The following diagram explains which systems are involved.

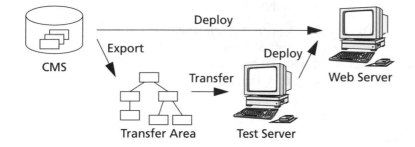

Editorial changes

1. An editor adds or updates content in the content management system (CMS).
2. An editor-in-chief reviews and publishes the content. Upon calling a function offered by the CMS, the new or modified content is deployed directly to the web server. The web server need not be restarted.

Structural changes

1. A programmer makes changes to the JSP programming within the templates used in the CMS.
2. Once the changes are finished, the programmer calls a function that exports the content from the CMS into a file system structure known as the transfer area.
3. The programmer invokes a process that transfers the contents onto the test server.
4. The programmer tests the changes with a web server that runs on the test machine.
5. Steps 1 to 4 are repeated until the tests are successful. The changes are now ready to be published to the web.
6. A web server administrator stops the web server process, transfers the modified content from the test machine to the web server, and re-starts the web server process.

Figure 10. Excerpt from a project document, organised differently

Readers can access information much faster in documents that follow the style of the second excerpt, which is taken from Project OpenDoors.

Agile documentation follows this approach and aims to produce better documents through the following techniques:

- The key idea is to provide documents with a useful structure that guides readers through the material, thereby helping them to obtain the information they need.

- The inclusion of meaningful diagrams can make documents a trigger for face-to-face communication.

- A reasonable dose of meta-information informs readers about the material they have in front of them, so that they can decide whether the material is for them and see how it relates to other project artefacts, for example the software that is being built.

This chapter begins with patterns that take a general look at the structure of documents, then moves on to patterns that suggest concrete elements you can use. Figure 11 provides an overview.

These patterns not only make documents more accessible to their readers, they also help authors write project documents more quickly. Adding information to a well-structured document is much easier than updating a complex literary artefact. A useful document structure paves the way for lightweight documents and to an agile documentation process.

Related to the way in which you structure your project documents is the writing style you use, though it is not covered by these patterns. Generally, a straightforward style will do your project documents good. If you're interested in style issues, I'd like to refer you to the body of literature. English readers will find *The Elements of Style* by William Strunk and E. B. White most useful – short, precise and to the point (Strunk White 1979). German readers might profit from Wolf Schneider's books (Schneider 1996, 1999).

Finally, I'd like to point out that the patterns in this chapter do not prescribe a specific writing style. Everybody has their own individual writing style, and this is fine. Instead, these patterns offer you some suggestions on how you can improve your documents by enhancing their structure and by making them more accessible to your readers.

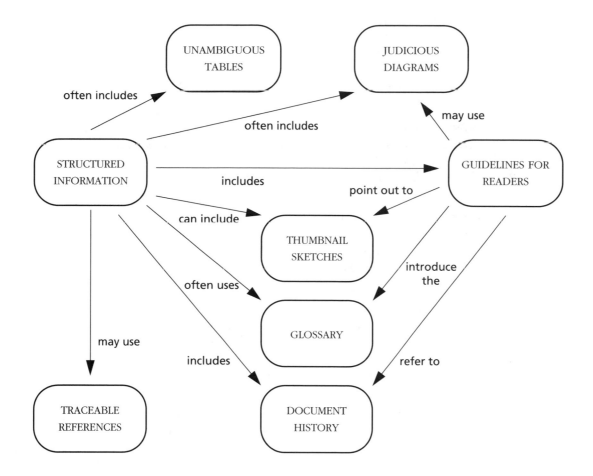

Figure 11. Patterns for structuring individual documents

Structured Information

Problem   **How can information be presented in an easily accessible way?**

Forces   Project documents have two types of readers. You might want to read a document from beginning to end, or you might be an occasional reader who is mainly interested in looking up information and who reads longer passages only when necessary. Ideally, project documents should allow both for sequential reading and for quick information retrieval, so serving both kinds of readers.

Robert Horn analysed written communication and found that humans can process structured information more quickly and more reliably than unstructured information (Horn 1989). Readers can retrieve information more easily when it is accurately classified and structured.

Experience shows that, indeed, poorly-structured documents often fail to serve their purpose with occasional readers. Occasional readers, when they look for specific information, are willing to browse through a document for a while, but give up when their search proves unsuccessful and assume the information isn't available.

This might suggest that project documents should be organised as hypertext, using hyperlinks to lead readers through the parts of a document that are relevant to them. However, we must bear in mind that documents must also allow for sequential reading, and that hypertext is counter-intuitive to reading from beginning to end. Enhancing a sequential text with a rich structure springs to mind. But to which degree should a document be structured?

A prominent psychological study gives us a hint. In 1956, the psychologist George A. Miller observed that people are generally able to identify and memorise about seven pieces of information at one time (Miller 1956). This observation can be applied to the overall structure of documents.[4] For example, a chapter consisting of significantly more than seven sections is difficult to handle for occasional readers who seek to memorise the document structure. On the other hand, a chapter consisting of significantly less than seven sections seems to be poorly structured. The same applies to the

---

4. Miller's rule of seven has often been misinterpreted and misused. The sidebar on page 67 explains why it can indeed be applied to the structure of project documents, as far as making documents accessible to occasional readers is concerned.

Sidebar: the magical number seven

George A. Miller's ground-breaking paper from 1956, *'The magical number seven, plus or minus two: Some limits on our capacity for processing information'* (Miller 1956), has been much referenced in the literature on both communication sciences and computer science.

Miller conducted a number of experiments that tested the short-term memory of the human brain. The experiments were based on a discrete set of stimuli in a linear, that is one-dimensional, order such as points on a line, pitches or loudnesses. People had to identify a randomly chosen stimulus.

The ratio of successful tests vs. the overall number of tests gets smaller as the set of stimuli gets larger. Miller observed that around a total of seven stimuli, the chances of accurate identification sink dramatically. This observation was independent of the type of stimulus – visual, acoustic or other.

Miller concluded that seven represents an upper limit on the human capacity for processing information, and claims of the number seven that there is 'some pattern governing its appearance'.

It is important to understand that this limit of seven applies:

- When the stimuli are in linear order, and
- When individual stimuli need to be identified

Miller's rule therefore doesn't say that a novel shouldn't have more than seven chapters. True, the chapters of a novel are in linear order, but why would someone want to identify an individual chapter?

Miller's rule doesn't apply to Web sites either, in the sense that a Web site shouldn't have more than seven pages. Users might have to identify an individual page from an entire site in order to retrieve some particular information. But then, Web sites aren't organised in a one-dimensional way.

Miller's rule does apply to typical documents from software projects. Because such documents are structured into chapters, sections and so on, they are organised in a one-dimensional order. And while some people read a document from beginning to end, occasional readers browse a document, read something here, and look for some other information somewhere else. Occasional readers can familiarise themselves with a document much more easily if the document structure – its chapters and sections – meets Miller's 'Rule of Seven'.

number of chapters in the entire document and the number of subsections to a section.

However, the rule of seven does not say anything about how deeply information should be structured. Chapters, sections and subsections are fairly normal, but what about sub-subsections? There is no general limit to the depth of structured documents, but it seems that most readers prefer documents to be structured no more than three levels deep.

Solution

Most project documents are best organised as sequential yet well-structured text. This begins with well-chosen chapters and sections, but may well extend to using textual building blocks consistently throughout a document.

Let's take a closer look at what this means.

- The first step is to organise documents with meaningful chapters, sections and perhaps subsections. Given such a structure, readers can access information in a document much more easily than if the structure was missing. The structure is most effective if it follows Miller's rule of seven: about seven chapters to a document, about seven sections to a chapter and so on.

- You can enhance the structure of your documents by taking a second step. Figure 12 illustrates a page that could be taken from a design document – a section that consists of five building blocks. What could these building blocks represent? For the sake of the argument, let's assume that the page describes a class, and that the building blocks represent the class name, an introductory text, a class diagram, an interface specification and a message sequence chart. You could then use sections that are structured in this way repeatedly all over the document, describing all classes consistently. A consistent structure for a class description is of course just one example, but a similar structure could be equally useful in many other kinds of documents.

Whether structuring sections into building blocks makes sense depends on the actual document, or whether a clear structure of chapters and sections is all you can, or want to, achieve. Either way, this pattern allows you to create a well-structured and evenly-balanced document.

Discussion

For a quick example, look back to Figure 9 and Figure 10. Figure 10 presents structured information, Figure 9 doesn't. The structure is exactly what makes

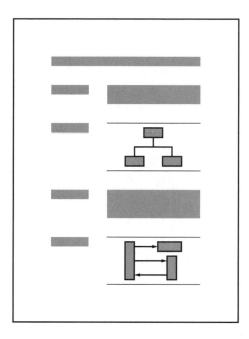

Figure 12. Structured information – a section consisting of five building blocks

the difference between the two documents, and it is clear that the structure adds to the readability displayed by Figure 10.

A prominent example of structured information is CRC cards (Beck Cunningham 1989). CRC cards provide a common structure to describe the responsibilities of the classes involved in a design. The consistent structure of the CRC cards makes CRC cards quick to follow and convenient to work with.

The pattern form used in this book is another example of structured information. Each pattern consists of five building blocks: its title, the problem, the forces, the solution and the discussion. The structure makes it easy for readers to identify which part of the pattern holds which type of information. Tags such as *problem*, *forces*, *solution* and *discussion* represent the meta-information that allows you, the reader, to classify the information that this book has in store for you.

An important idea behind structuring information is that the use of diagrams and tables can make a document's structure more visible. This visibility helps readers perceive the contents of a document. Figure 12 illustrates this with two building blocks consisting of a diagram, and Figure 10 gives a concrete example. In general, JUDICIOUS DIAGRAMS can provide excellent overviews, while UNAMBIGUOUS TABLES present systematic information. In addition, you can enhance the structure of your documents by means of layout and typography, especially with CAREFUL USE OF TYPE VARIATIONS and through CAREFUL RULING AND SHADING.

All these ideas about structuring documents beg the question of which sections and subsections you actually need. Naturally, there is no general answer to this question, but there are several patterns that address this issue. When you set up the overall structure of a document, be sure to include GUIDELINES FOR READERS and a DOCUMENT HISTORY. Often you'll need a GLOSSARY, as well as a section with TRACEABLE REFERENCES to other documents. When it comes to more fine-grained structuring, THUMBNAIL SKETCHES added to the sections of your document give quicker access for occasional readers.

A final remark on the rule of seven. When you structure a document, you should always keep the overall principle of presenting FOCUSED INFORMATION in the back of your mind. There is no point in setting up seven chapters if you don't have enough material for seven chapters. Creating a chapter or a section is sensible only when you can define its focus. So take the rule of seven with a grain of salt.[5]

Judicious Diagrams

Problem   **How can authors provide an overview of structures and processes in a convenient way?**

Forces   Structures and processes play an important role in software engineering. The structure of a software system describes how the system is organised and how it is composed from smaller parts. Processes describe the dynamic side of software – interaction and state-driven behaviour, among other things.

---

5. For example, the number of chapters in this book is at the lower end of the range that the rule of seven suggests, while the number of patterns in each chapter tends to be at (or even a little beyond) the upper end.

If we look at common modelling techniques, we see that diagrams are frequently used to describe structures and processes. UML, for example, has class diagrams, message sequence diagrams, use case diagrams and others (Rumbaugh Jacobsen Booch 1998, Fowler 2000).

This is not really surprising – we all know that one picture can be worth more than a thousand words. Diagrams speak to our intuition.

There is also scientific evidence that diagrams help readers perceive information. For example, Edward Tufte's books on the visual representation of information give an impressive account (Tufte 1997, 2001).

Moreover, there is a subtle psychological reason why diagrams are sometimes better suited for explaining material to readers. Diagrams allow us to illustrate information in a two-dimensional way, which increases its comprehensibility (Miller 1956).

There are more points in favour of diagrams. Readers tend to get bored with long, monotonous texts. Texts that include diagrams are much less monotonous. Diagrams serve as eye-catchers that quickly attract readers, and also help readers memorise information. Readers often associate a text with the included diagrams, so that when they browse the text in search of specific information a while later, the diagrams give them orientation (Tufte 1997, 2001).

Yet diagrams lack the nuances that language offers. Unless diagrams are very complicated, they contain less detail than text. Complicated diagrams, however, lose much of the charm that make simple, 'in-your-face' diagrams appeal to us.

This leaves us in the dilemma that diagrams alone, however valuable they may be, cannot provide comprehensive information, but often leave detailed questions unanswered.

Solution   **Diagrams can provide excellent overviews, while an accompanying text explains details to the extent that is necessary.**

Good diagrams complement the text. A diagram often describes a whole and its parts, as well as the relationships and dependencies that hold between the parts. The surrounding text can refer to the diagram and can dig deeper into the subject matter.

There is a wide range of things that can be described very well through diagrams. The following list isn't complete, but gives you a good idea of the different kinds of diagrams, some of which are well known from UML (Rumbaugh Jacobsen Booch 1998, Fowler 2000):

- Architecture overviews

- Class diagrams

- Interaction diagrams

- Activity diagrams

- State diagrams

- Deployment diagrams

Of course, you shouldn't clutter your documents with unnecessary diagrams. If a diagram isn't meaningful, go without it. But whenever you write a document, keep asking yourself whether there is some information that would be better expressed visually.

The best diagrams are often those that are clear and simple. Ideally, a diagram uses only a fairly small number of graphical elements, which, if necessary, should be explained in a legend. Sometimes even a perfectly informal whiteboard drawing captured by a digital camera makes an excellent diagram (Cockburn 2001, Ambler 2002).

Discussion   Diagrams are prominent in good documentation anyway, but they are particularly important in an agile context. Agile documentation gives preference to communicating THE BIG PICTURE over writing down long lists of details, so a diagram is often the method of choice. Diagrams can get an idea across, diagrams can get a discussion started, diagrams promote communication.

Because diagrams are such good eye-catchers, they can increase the efficiency of STRUCTURED INFORMATION. If you choose to organise your document with the help of a distinct structure, the inclusion of diagrams can turn out to be helpful, as Figure 13 illustrates.

The GUIDELINES FOR READERS can almost always make good use of a diagram to give an overview and to explain how the sections of a document relate to each other. In a similar vein, but on a larger scale, a project's introductory document can use a diagram to give an overview of the entire documentation and to explain how individual documents relate to each other. In other words, a diagram can visualise the DOCUMENT LANDSCAPE.

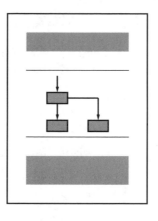

Figure 13. Text mixed with a diagram

Unambiguous Tables

Problem   **How can authors present systematic information in a precise way?**

Forces   Systematic information is common in software projects. In a world where analytical thinking plays a major role, systematic information becomes an essential tool of the trade.

Think of all the lists you keep: the list of all modules of a system, of all interface methods, of all error codes, of all data types, of all work packages, just to name a few. More examples of systematic information are also found in many projects: classification schemes, steps in a process, mappings and so on.

Such systematic information is often subject to documentation. Team members, however, aren't interested in reading a long text when all they want to know could easily be presented as a list entry.

Using tables to present systematic information is the obvious choice. Tables are clear and direct. Similar to diagrams, tables profit from the psychological advantage that they are two-dimensional. The two dimensions are represented by the rows and columns, which allow for arrangements that sequential text cannot render.

Similarly to diagrams, tables can make a text less monotonous. If only for the typographical variety, tables can attract the reader's attention easily.

However, tables also have a disadvantage that they share with diagrams. Tables offer only little linguistic expressiveness. If material requires an argument for its explanation, more than can fit into a table cell, a table alone cannot be sufficient.

Solution   **Tables offer a compact format for the concise and unambiguous presentation of information.**

The following list doesn't claim completeness, but gives you a few examples of systematic materials that can very well be presented in tables:

- Interface specifications (function name, signature, abstract, error codes)
- Lists of classes, methods, data types, etc.
- Error handling tables (error code, reaction)
- Comparison of the pros and cons of a design option
- Different steps to be taken in a process or an activity
- Work packages and their deadlines

The more self-contained a table is, the easier it is to understand. Ideally, the headings for the rows and columns give the readers all the information necessary to understand the table. Background information on what is presented in the table will often have to go into the surrounding text, however.

Discussion   Tables are often found in the context of STRUCTURED INFORMATION, as they add to the document structure. Figure 14 illustrates this.

Tables can be used to implement the SEPARATION OF DESCRIPTION AND EVALUATION, for example by devoting one column to observations and another to comments, or by placing facts in a table and interpretations in the surrounding text.

The variety in the layout has been mentioned as one of the advantages that tables offer. CAREFUL RULING AND SHADING allows you to produce tables that look good from a typographical point of view.

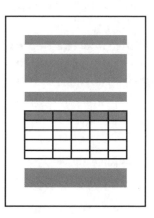

Figure 14. A clearly-structured table between surrounding text

Guidelines for Readers

Problem   **How can potential readers be informed whether they should read a document, and if so, on which parts they should focus?**

Forces   People who are involved in a software project are typically occupying different roles that have different information needs. A document can be important for someone and completely irrelevant to someone else.

Moreover, several people can read the same document with different intentions. Some readers might only want to get an overview of the topic, others might be looking for some specific detail, while a third group might want to read the document in its entirety.

In addition, some documents require that readers have read other documents previously, or otherwise be familiar with certain material. Potential readers therefore need to be informed of the prerequisites for understanding a document.

There might also be dependencies within the document itself. The chapters of some documents are relatively independent of each other, and readers can concentrate on the chapters in which they are interested. But sometimes readers need to go through one chapter before they're able to understand another.

Solution   **Some brief guidelines at the beginning of each document can inform potential readers of the purpose the document serves and explain how different groups of readers should approach the document.**

The guidelines must prevent readers from studying documents that don't contain the information they require. They must also prevent readers from going through a complete document when only parts of it are relevant.

To do this, the guidelines must answer the following questions:

- Who should read the document?

- What is inside, and what is outside the scope of the document?

- How is the document organised?

- What are the dependencies between the different chapters of the document? Is there a specific order in which to read the chapters?

- What are the relationships to other documents? Are there other documents that readers are expected to have read previously?

- How can readers get a quick overview of the contents?

- Is the document complete, or does it describe a work in progress? Are updates to be expected? If the document is an update of a former version, which parts have changed?

Discussion   However the guidelines for readers appear in detail, they are meant to welcome the TARGET READERS to a document. They explicitly say who the TARGET READERS are, address them, and let them know how to use the document.

A diagram (see JUDICIOUS DIAGRAMS) is often the method of choice for describing the overall organisation of a document, as well as the dependencies between its chapters. The diagram can serve as a road map for readers when they browse through the document to find the parts of interest.

Pointing out to the readers how they can get a quick overview is particularly easy when the individual chapters of the document are provided with THUMB-NAIL SKETCHES. It's also useful to refer to the DOCUMENT HISTORY, as it informs potential readers of the document's status and of changes between previous versions.

Thumbnail Sketches

Problem   **How can readers get an overview of the topics dealt with in a document?**

Forces   It is difficult for readers to find what they want in a document that contains a lot of information. Guidelines can tell readers what to expect from the document, but cannot say where to look for any specific detail.

A clear structure of chapters, sections and subsections makes it easier for readers to find particular information, yet a clear structure alone may not be sufficient to allow readers to retrieve information quickly.

Quick information retrieval is necessary, however. Ideally, readers can browse through a document at a high level, and dig deeper whenever they feel that some part of the document is particularly relevant to them.

Gerald Weinberg explains in *The Psychology of Computer Programming*: '... different users of the documentation will need different levels of detail in the information they extract. The highest level should be just sufficiently detailed to tell the user whether or not he will be able to read the documents.' (Weinberg 1998)

Solution   **Thumbnail sketches provide brief descriptions of the sections of a document, including the section's general goals, as well as its major ideas.**

A document that supplies thumbnail sketches allows for sequential reading at different levels of detail. After reading a thumbnail sketch, readers can decide whether they would like to go deeper or whether to move on to the next section.

There are two ways to set up thumbnail sketches:

- You can let each section begin with some kind of abstract or summary.

- You can choose a few paragraphs from each section, though not necessarily at the beginning, and use those as thumbnail sketches. Layout techniques can be used for their identification.

Both techniques preserve the sequential order of the text, so that people can read the document from beginning to end if they want to, while other readers can focus on the thumbnails for a quick scan.

Discussion   This pattern builds upon the idea of STRUCTURED INFORMATION. When you use a common structure consistently throughout a document, thumbnail sketches appear repeatedly at the same place within a section, where they can easily be identified.

This effect is strengthened by the CAREFUL USE OF TYPE VARIATIONS, for example by the use of boldface or italics for the thumbnail sketches.

Consider this book. It uses a pattern form consistently. For each pattern, the problem section and the first paragraph of the solution section form a thumbnail sketch. You can find out the main idea behind each pattern without having to read its every detail. The boldface parts give you a first impression: you can go deeper, but you don't have to.

Finally, since thumbnail sketches help readers navigate through a document, you will probably want to mention them in the GUIDELINES FOR READERS.

Traceable References

Problem   **How can documents be linked to each other?**

Forces   Each document is supposed to focus on one topic. However, no document can be seen in isolation. There are always related topics that need to be understood beforehand or related documents that provide additional information. As a consequence, almost all documents must include references to other documents.

But what happens if a referenced document isn't available to the reader? After all, the reader is supposed to look up that reference if more information is required. A reference to a document that's unavailable isn't worth much and could just as well be left out.

Solution   **A document should include references to other documents only if readers can obtain those documents without much effort.**

The following rules of thumb are useful:

- References to other documents in the same project are obviously fine.

- References to documents from other projects are fine only so long as those documents can be distributed among the team. There shouldn't be any references to documents that are restricted to internal use or that underlie a non-disclosure agreement.

- Almost all organisations have libraries that contain the standard literature of software engineering. References to such books and journals are easy to follow.

- Scientific publications that aren't readily available are a different matter. References to such sources are often difficult to track down, and are therefore inappropriate.

Within a project, it is useful not only to refer to a related document, but also to point out to the readers explicitly where they can find the document.

Discussion You might ask whether references can be avoided altogether. The FOCUSED INFORMATION pattern provides the answer. Your aim should be to produce self-contained documents that aren't cluttered with references to other documents. However, in order to give each document a clear focus and to avoid large overlaps between documents, you cannot avoid references completely.

If you aren't sure whether you should use a reference or include material, the inclusion of THUMBNAIL SKETCHES may represent a good compromise. This solution avoids overlaps to a large extent, although not entirely, while still adding to the document's self-containedness.

The appropriateness of references also depends on who the TARGET READERS of a document are. Team members normally have access to a different set of documents to customers, and so have team members as opposed to managers. When referencing other documents, you need to take this into account.

Electronic documents can use hyperlinks to reference related documents. In this way, readers can navigate from one referenced document to the other. This is a nice technique for documents that are intended for on-line use. However, many project documents are intended to be printed, so hyperlinks are only of limited use. (See also the discussion on READER-FRIENDLY MEDIA.)

Glossary

Problem **How can authors make sure that readers understand the vocabulary used in a document?**

Forces Technical terms often occur in the documentation produced for a software project. Design documents in particular cannot do without terms that are specific to the technology used. While some technical terms more or less belong to the standard vocabulary of software engineering, readers might be unfamiliar with others.

Moreover, many software projects use terminology that is specific to the customer's organisation or the application domain, and not all readers can be expected to be familiar with it. Domain-specific terms can be a hurdle, especially to new team members.

If you explain all these terms wherever they occur, however, you scatter explanations all over the text. This carries the additional danger that in different places you offer slightly different explanations, which is not going to make your documents more accurate.

Moreover, an explanation somewhere in the text is fine for people who read the document from beginning to end, but is not really helpful for occasional readers who browse the document in search of a definition or explanation.

Solution   **A glossary can explain technical terms as well as the terms specific to the application domain.**

Most project documents can profit from a glossary. The more technical documents will mainly require explanations of technical terms, while requirement specifications rely heavily on the vocabulary of the application domain.

In a first step, setting up a glossary is easy:

* The glossary lists all specific terms relevant to the document in alphabetical order.

* Each entry presents a definition or explanation that is understood by the team members, and perhaps includes a reference to further information sources.

If a project requires several documents, and these documents have overlapping glossaries, redundant effort is the consequence. To avoid this, you can use a central glossary and reference it from project documents.

Discussion   Giving definitions of domain-specific terms may not be easy. Regarding the SPECIFICATION AS A JOINT EFFORT helps, as you can almost always obtain good explanations from the customer.

Readers must be aware of a glossary if they are to use it. In particular, if you use a central glossary, the fact that the glossary exists at all is not always obvious. Mentioning the glossary in the GUIDELINES FOR READERS helps.

A large project might consider a glossary tool – essentially a small database of technical terms and terms from the application domain – that you can use to extract a list of those terms you need in a special context. Such a tool manages redundancy between the glossaries of several documents. It should, however, be chosen only if managing redundancy manually isn't quicker. There's no point in using a tool if the tool doesn't make things easier.

Document History

Problem

How can confusion be avoided between versions of a document?

Forces

At the beginning of a project not all the details of what needs to be documented are known. The project will evolve and will undergo change, and so do the project documents. Documents are going to be created, updated and extended, perhaps many times.

But even documents that are updated regularly can get out of sync with what they describe. You cannot update documentation at the same rate as that at which the software progresses, otherwise you would be updating the documentation on a daily basis. The consequence is that in between updates, documentation isn't quite up to date.

This isn't a huge problem, as long as readers are aware that what they read might be slightly out of date, and as long as they know that in the meantime the software may have been developed further.

Solution

A document history can explain the differences to previous versions of a document, and can relate the document to versions of the software it describes.

A document history is essentially a table with an entry for each new version. It is extended as the document evolves. Each entry is typically associated with a version number for the document, and includes the following information:

- The author of that version.

- A brief list of the changes that were made since the last version of the document was released.

- If the document describes actual software, the version of the software to which the document refers.

This way, readers can understand how a document has evolved during the course of a project.

Discussion   Maintaining a document history only makes sense in the presence of CONTINUING DOCUMENTATION. The document history is not meant as an excuse for documents never being updated, but serves to bridge the natural lag between versions.

The document history can be part of the GUIDELINES FOR READERS, or should otherwise be referred to from there.

You might choose to store earlier versions of important documents in a DOCUMENT ARCHIVE, especially in larger projects. Some archives are capable of adding entries to a document history automatically, though normally this is possible only with plain text files.

Experience Reports

Let's look at how the patterns in this chapter were applied in the documentation of some of our example projects.

Document   structure   I'd like to begin with the idea of STRUCTURED INFORMATION. This idea was present in the documentation of most projects, but some documents demonstrate the usefulness of structured information particularly well. Let's go back for a moment to the experiment at the beginning of this chapter. Figure 10 on page 63 contains a page from the deployment description that Project OpenDoors produced. Figure 9 on page 62 contains a page I mocked up to demonstrate the difference. Figure 10 features STRUCTURED INFORMATION, whereas Figure 9 doesn't.

There are more examples of how adding structure makes a document more readable. The design document from Project Navigator defines a text structure that is uniformly applied to the design description of all components. Figure 15 shows the description of one such component. Each component description features a brief overview statement, an interface description, a description of the component's internals, as well as a UML diagram. The UML diagrams grasp the functionality of all these components: they are JUDICIOUS DIAGRAMS.

The usage concept from Project Persistor is targeted towards the users of the data access layer framework. The usage concept explains how each interface

Navigation Box

The navigation box is a user interface control that takes input from the user and adjusts the details of the map currently under display.

The control's visual appearance is that of a small box, with arrows symbolising the functions for moving the displayed area, and knobs symbolising the zoom for displaying different levels of detail. See the GUI specification for an example screenshot.

The class NavigationBox implements the interface for user interface controls.

Interface description

```
class NavigationBox

// This method shifts the area of the map that is currently
// under display, either upwards, downwards, to the left, or
// to the right. It takes the desired direction as a
// parameter.
public void move (unsigned short direction);

// This method changes the level of detail that is shown.
// Depending on the parameter that is passed to the method,
// the display either zooms into the map by one step, or
// zooms out.
public void zoom (boolean zoom-in);
```

Class diagram

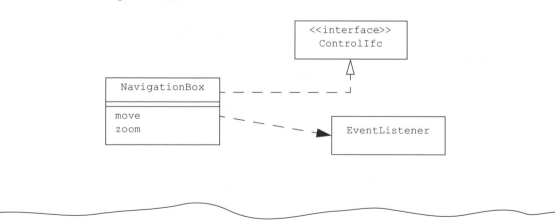

Figure 15. Project Navigator: structured information applied to a design document

4.2.1   Adding an object

```
addObject ()

        IN objectType                : DT-TYPE
        IN fullKey                   : DT-KEY
        IN entryDate                 : DT-DATE
        IN processNumber             : DT-NR
```

Preconditions:

Function:

  **The data access layer provides an initial version of a new object,
  according to the entry date and the process number passed on to it as
  parameters. Upon initialisation, the new object may still be incomplete;
  components can be added successively. The new object's state is
  "pending".**

  The key that is passed to this function as an input parameter is a logical key,
  which may or may not carry application-specific information. It is normally
  generated by a specific module that all applications can use.

  In case the specified key has been used previously for adding an object, an error
  code is returned.

  The process number is generated by the workflow management system.

Return Codes:

RC-OK	The object has been entered and initialised correctly.
RC-KEY	The specified logical key isn't available.
RC-DB	The database is not available.
RC-PARAMETER	The entry date or the process number are illegal.

Figure 16. Project Persistor: a well-structured document

method can be applied. Figure 16 shows the description of one such method. The interface description consists of building blocks for the signature, the list of parameters, preconditions, a description, and the error codes. Throughout all method descriptions, the signature, the list of parameters and the first paragraph of the description form THUMBNAIL SKETCHES for each function. The error codes for each function are presented using UNAMBIGUOUS TABLES.

Useful elements

Let's take a closer look at the usage concept from Project Persistor, as it features several of the useful elements the patterns in this chapter suggest should be included in a document. Figure 17 shows the DOCUMENT HISTORY taken from one of the first pages of the document. It explains the document status, the changes that have been made to the document in the past, who made these changes and why.

History

Version	Status	Date	Authors	Remark
0.1	draft	1999-Jun-19	A. Rüping	First draft • architectural overview • using the interface
0.2	draft	1999-Jun-24	A. Rüping	A few small changes
0.3	draft	1999-Jun-30	A. Rüping	Changes after internal review: • state model added • example on versioning added
0.4	draft	1999-Aug-06	A. Rüping	A few minor changes: • API definitions • logical transactions
1.0	released	1999-Aug-30	A. Rüping	Changes after external review
2.0	released	1999-Oct-22	A. Rüping	Update reflecting the release of the new framework version

Figure 17. Project Persistor: a document history

Figure 18 shows the GUIDELINES FOR READERS, which, in the original document, appear at the beginning of the introduction. They directly address the readers through a few introductory words. Although they are quite short, they make clear who should read the document and how the document is organised.

Guidelines for Readers

This document describes the usage of the data access layer named ████ that was developed in the ███ project performed jointly by ███ and ███. The document is meant to be used by team members of all ██████ projects.

The data access layer is to be used by all applications currently under development. At this point, these are the new health insurance system and the new customer system. More projects are expected to start soon; they will use the data access layer too.

To allow the data access layer to be used by several projects, it has been designed as a framework. This framework can (and must) be configured to reflect the specifics of a project that uses it, in particular its data model.

This document describes how to configure and to use the data access layer framework (release 4.0 / 2000-June-28). We begin with a sketch of the basic concepts the data access layer uses, and then briefly describe its architecture. The main part of this document is an API description which explains each function separately. Guidelines for the configuration follow. We conclude with a few hints that explain how to use the framework along with some examples from the health insurance project.

Figure 18. Project Persistor: guidelines for readers

Figure 19 shows an excerpt from the GLOSSARY that appears in an appendix at the end of the usage concept. It briefly explains the special terms used in the document, including both technical terms and vocabulary specific to the application domain.

Finally, Figure 20 shows the list of references from the usage document. They are TRACEABLE REFERENCES, as team members can easily obtain the information

Glossary

state	The data access layer allows objects to be in different states: active, pending, and inactive. In the application domain these states match the modes in which an insurance contract can be: valid, under revision, offer.
logical transaction	A logical transaction consists of the entirety of steps to be performed together: an atomic use case. If one step leads to an error or is interrupted, the previous steps need do be undone.
database transaction	A database transaction consists of a sequence of write / update / delete commands that are either committed to the database (commit) or ignored (rollback). This is the mechanism that a database offers to implement logical transactions. In the data access layer, logical transaction may consist of several database transactions. The data access layer uses caching mechanisms to make sure a logical rollback is possible.

Figure 19. Project Persistor: a glossary

References

[*MS]   Management Summary, "~/architecture/summary.doc".

[*RS]   Requirement Specification, "~/specification/requirements.doc".

[*AD]   Architecture & Design Overview, "~/architecture/architecture+design.doc".

[GoF]   Erich Gamma, Richard Helm, Ralph Johnson, John Vlissides. "Design Patterns", Addison-Wesley, 1995.

Figure 20. Project Persistor: list of references

to which they refer: a couple of other project documents and a readily available book on software design.

Diagrams and tables

In all the project documents we have looked at in the experience reports, we have already come across several diagrams that proved extremely useful. THE BIG PICTURE documents described in Figure 6, Figure 7 and Figure 8 (pages 52–56) all make use of JUDICIOUS DIAGRAMS, and so did the design concept from Project Navigator (Figure 15). I think it's easy for you to imagine many more examples – you have probably come across many useful diagrams in your everyday practice.

Let me give you just one more example. Figure 21 is again taken from Project Persistor, and while the details of what the diagrams describe are irrelevant, the project report explains why the diagrams were so useful to the team.

Project Persistor: getting the idea across with a diagram

Two-dimensional history is a concept common in financial information systems that separates the moment in which a value is entered into a system from the moment that value becomes effective. The concept features some algorithmic complexity, and explaining it in words is an intricate matter, but diagrams help a lot. Two axes represent effectiveness on one hand and known-at time on the other (Figure 21). Time intervals appear as bounded areas on a plane. Because the framework used two-dimensional history a lot, the usage concept included several diagrams that explained the concept. After reading the usage concept, someone from the customer's team said: 'I never quite understood what two-dimensional history is all about. It's so incredibly abstract. But now that I have seen these diagrams, I've finally understood.' Several other team members expressed similar experiences.

Not only diagrams add structure to a text and make it less monotonous – the same is true for tables. Again, I'm sure you can think of many examples, so I'll only present two here.

Figure 22 shows an excerpt from a table that lists the requirements placed on the Web content management system in Project Contentis. Separate columns are reserved for unique numbering, the actual requirements and their priorities. Without a table, the assignment of priorities to requirements would not have been nearly as clear as it is here.

Figure 23 shows an excerpt from the table illustrating the characteristics of various insurance products that was used to document the re-engineering

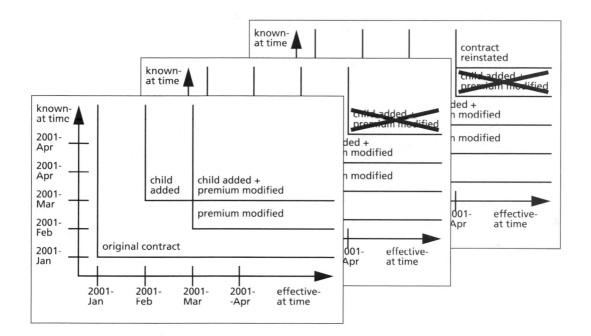

Figure 21. Project Persistor: diagrams explaining a special kind of versioning

effort in Project Extricate. It is clear that you, as reader of this book, may not understand the contents of this table, but I think you can gauge how important it was to the project. For all insurance products, the table clearly states their properties and demonstrates why we speak of UNAMBIGUOUS TABLES. The table was of great use to the project team, as the project report explains.

1.3.3	Which publication channels are supported?	B
1.4	Templates	
1.4.1	Is there a template editor?	A
1.4.2	Can templates be organised in a hierarchical fashion?	C
1.4.3	Can templates inherit features from parent templates?	C
1.4.4	Is the number of templates limited?	A
1.4.5	Do the templates offer support for HTML frames?	B
1.4.6	Can templates include code, such as JSP?	A
1.5	Import / Export	
1.5.1	Which import mechanisms does the CMS provide (text, graphics, XML)?	A
1.5.2	Which print formats (PDF etc.) can be imported?	A
1.6	Versioning	
1.6.1	Is there support for branching?	B

Figure 22. Project Contentis: a table used to prioritise software requirements

Project Extricate: information condensed into one table

Specifying all insurance products and their properties to the last detail would have been incredibly complex. It soon turned out, however, that what the team needed most was an overview of all the products and their properties – a list or a table, something systematic. As a consequence, the team developed a huge spreadsheet in which various kinds of properties were assigned to various kinds of insurance products.

This spreadsheet table was set up first at the beginning of the project, but was maintained and updated for almost two years. Both developers and customers used the spreadsheet in meetings whenever they discussed how product properties could be modelled in the new system. There was more documentation than just this spreadsheet, documentation that provided more details, but it was the spreadsheet that was used in many discussions and was most useful.

product	old key	new key	type	subtype	opening date	closing date	status	generation	number of insured persons	supplement	supplement possible	supplement mandatory	premium type	dynamics	flexible premium	reduced premium	flexible termination	policy mode	children	funds
L1S	11	0001	LFE	STD	1948-01	1955-05	C	1	X	N	N	N	R	N	N	N	N	I	P	COV
L1R	12	0002	LFE	RSK	1948-01	1955-05	C	1	1	N	N	N	R	N	N	N	N	I	P	COV
L1F	13	0003	LFE	FIX	1948-01	1955-05	C	1	1	N	N	N	R	N	N	N	N	I	S	COV
LG	19	0004	LFE	STD	1948-01	1955-05	C	1	1	N	N	Y	R	N	N	Y	N	G	P	COV
L2S	21	0005	LFE	STD	1955-05	1970-01	C	2	X	N	N	N	P	N	N	N	N	I	P	COV
L2R	22	0006	LFE	RSK	1955-05	1970-01	C	2	1	N	N	N	P	N	N	N	N	I	P	COV
L2F	23	0007	LFE	FIX	1955-05	1970-01	C	2	1	N	N	N	P	N	N	N	N	I	S	COV
X	29	0008	LFE	STD	1955-05	1970-01	C	2	1	N	N	Y	R	N	N	Y	N	G	P	COV
L3S	51	0009	LFE	STD	1970-01	1990-10	C	3	1	N	Y	N	P	N	Y	N	Y	I	P	COV
L3R	52	0010	LFE	RSK	1970-01	1990-10	C	3	1	N	Y	N	P	N	N	N	N	I	P	COV
L3F	53	0011	LFE	FIX	1970-01	1990-10	C	3	1	N	Y	N	P	N	N	N	N	I	P	COV
L4S	61	0012	LFE	STD	1990-10		O	4	1	N	Y	N	P	P	Y	N	Y	I	P	COV
L4R	62	0013	LFE	RSK	1990-10		O	4	1	N	Y	N	P	P	N	N	N	I	P	COV
L4F	63	0014	LFE	FIX	1990-10		O	4	1	N	Y	N	P	P	N	N	N	I	P	COV
LF	70	0015	LFE	STD	1999-01		C	5	1	N	N	N	R	P	Y	N	Y	I	P	FND
P1	14	0016	PEN	IMM	1948-01	1957-01	C	1	1	N	N	N	R	N	N	N	N	I	P	COV
P2	24	0017	PEN	IMM	1957-01	1963-07	C	2	1	N	N	N	R	N	N	N	N	I	P	COV
P3	34	0018	PEN	IMM	1963-07	1970-01	C	2	1	N	N	N	R	N	N	N	N	I	P	COV
P3D	36	0019	PEN	DEL	1963-07	1970-01	C	2	1	N	N	N	P	N	N	N	N	I	P	COV
P4	54	0020	PEN	IMM	1970-01	1990-10	C	3	1	N	N	N	R	N	N	N	N	I	P	COV
P4D	56	0021	PEN	DEL	1970-01	1990-10	C	3	1	N	Y	N	P	N	N	N	N	I	P	COV
P5	64	0022	PEN	IMM	1990-10		O	4	1	N	N	N	R	P	N	N	N	I	P	COV
P5D	66	0023	PEN	DEL	1990-10		O	4	1	N	Y	N	P	P	N	N	N	I	P	COV
I1	15	0024	INV	MAIN	1948-01	1952-07	C	1	1	N	N	N	R	N	N	N	N	I	P	COV
IG	18	0025	INV	MAIN	1948-01	1952-07	C	1	1	Y	N	N	R	N	N	Y	N	G	P	COV
I2	25	0026	INV	MAIN	1952-07	1970-01	C	2	1	N	N	N	R	N	N	N	N	I	P	COV
I3	55	0027	INV	MAIN	1970-01	1990-10	C	3	1	N	N	N	R	N	N	N	N	I	P	COV
I3S	57	0028	INV	SUP	1970-01	1990-10	C	3	1	N	N	N	R	N	N	N	N	I	P	COV
I4	65	0029	INV	MAIN	1990-10		O	4	1	N	N	N	R	P	N	N	N	I	P	COV
I4S	67	0030	INV	SUP	1990-10		O	4	1	Y	N	N	R	P	N	N	N	I	P	COV

Figure 23. Project Extricate: a table summarising insurance product properties

3 Layout and Typography

Consistency and repetition establish pattern, which is an important aspect of order [...]. As experienced readers, we have learned to anticipate and expect pattern.

Suzanne West (West 1990)

In a book on agile documentation, a chapter dealing with layout and typography had better begin with an explanation. I can almost hear people exclaim: 'What do layout and typography have to do with an agile approach? Do they even matter?'

Yes, they do matter, though in a rather subtle way. Most readers are blissfully unaware of what it is that makes a document look good. There are factors that determine the quality of the layout, and the quality of the layout has an influence on the legibility of a document that is not to be ignored.

So what is the connection to being agile? Agile documentation suggests that you focus on documents that are necessary, and make sure that the necessary documents become high-quality documents. High legibility is one aspect of that quality.

You may argue that project documents don't require the same quality standards with respect to layout as do printed books, and this is of course correct. In an agile project documents cannot go through a lengthy layout process: other things are more important. Our goal must be to find a *quick and easy way* to produce documents with a high standard of legibility.

Let me support the significance of layout and typography with the following two points.

- Typography is an old art. The art of printing books dates back many centuries, gaining momentum in 1454, when Johannes Gutenberg invented printing using reusable letter forms. Typesetting rules have been developed and have matured since then. People wouldn't have spent so much time on typography if it didn't have any effect on legibility.

- Research underpins the significance of layout and typography. Miles Tinker conducted endless experiments in the middle of the last century and proved that bad typography slows down reading significantly. His findings are summarised in his book on the *Legibility of Print* (Tinker 1963). A study done in 2000 revealed that typography had an influence on the quality of proposals to a major funding agency and the percentage of successful proposals (Berleant 2000).

Still unconvinced? Look at the pages shown in Figure 24 and Figure 25. Both pages contain the same material. Which would you rather read? All aesthetics aside, which page do you think allows you to receive information more quickly and more reliably?

I think it's clear that the second page is much more legible than the first, and that layout and typography is what makes the difference between the two.

Fortunately, the road ahead of us on our way to a layout like that of Figure 25 isn't too rough – it requires less work than one might at first think. We can obtain a reasonably good layout for our project documents with quite little effort, and this is what the patterns in this chapter are about.

There are three reasons why little effort is needed to significantly improve the document layout:

1. A fairly small set of patterns can do a lot of good. The 80–20 rule applies: 80 percent of the advantages typography offers can be obtained by using about 20 percent of all typographical techniques available. Following an agile attitude, let's focus on the patterns that describe these techniques.

2. The patterns in this chapter can easily be implemented on most word processors.

3. Not everyone in the team needs to be concerned with these patterns. It is highly recommended that a project, or even an organisation, use DOCUMENT

- 20 -

4.2.1 ADDING AN OBJECT

```
addObject ()

     IN objectType          : DT-TYPE
     IN fullKey             : DT-KEY
     IN entryDate           : DT-DATE
     IN processNumber       : DT-NR
```

Preconditions:
none

Function:

The data access layer provides an initial version of a new object according to the entry date and the process number passed on to it as parameters. Upon initialisation, the new object may still be incomplete; components can be added successively. The new object's state is "pending".

The key that is passed to this function as an input parameter is a logical key, which may or may not carry application-specific information. It is normally generated by a specific module that all applications can use.

In case the specified key has been used previously for adding an object, an error code is returned.

The process number is generated by the workflow management system.

Return Codes:

RC-OK	The object has been entered and initialised correctly.
RC-KEY	The specified logical key isn't available.
RC-DB	The database is not available.
RC-PARAMETER	The entry date or the process number are illegal.

4.2.2 DELETING AN OBJECT

```
deleteObject ()

     IN objectType          : DT-TYPW
     IN fullKey             : DT-KEY
     IN deletionDate        : DT-DATE
     IN processNumber       : DT-NR
```

Preconditions:
the object has previously been added

Function:

Figure 24. Page layout: one variation

- 20 -

4.2.1 Adding an object

```
addObject ()

        IN objectType              : DT-TYPE
        IN fullKey                 : DT-KEY
        IN entryDate               : DT-DATE
        IN processNumber           : DT-NR
```

Preconditions:

    none

Function:

The data access layer provides an initial version of a new object according to the entry date and the process number passed on to it as parameters. Upon initialisation, the new object may still be incomplete; components can be added successively. The new object's state is "pending".

The key that is passed to this function as an input parameter is a logical key, which may or may not carry application-specific information. It is normally generated by a specific module that all applications can use.

In case the specified key has been used previously for adding an object, an error code is returned.

The process number is generated by the workflow management system.

Return Codes:

RC-OK	The object has been entered and initialised correctly.
RC-KEY	The specified logical key isn't available.
RC-DB	The database is not available.
RC-PARAMETER	The entry date or the process number are illegal.

4.2.2 Deleting an object

```
deleteObject ()

        IN objectType              : DT-TYPE
        IN fullKey                 : DT-KEY
        IN deletionDate            : DT-DATE
        IN processNumber           : DT-NR
```

Figure 25. Page layout: another variation

TEMPLATES to form the basis of all project documents. Once these templates have been designed according to the patterns on layout and typography, the project documents inherit the attractive layout of the templates. Individual authors find elementary typesetting rules already established before they begin to work on a document. All it then takes is a little discipline in using the features that the word processor offers.

Figure 26 gives an overview of the patterns from which the legibility of your project documents can profit. Reading your documents will be significantly more comfortable. The patterns ensure that the layout is adequate, if not perfect.

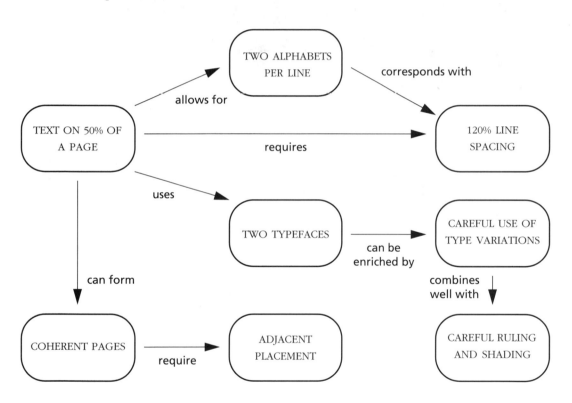

Figure 26. Patterns for layout and typography

There are, of course, many more typographical rules, and interested readers are invited to consult the rich body of literature on typography for more guidelines (Gulbins Kahrmann 1992, Tinker 1963, West 1990). But to obtain project documents that are reasonably well designed and which offer a high degree of legibility, the patterns in this chapter, combined with a good dose of common sense, will suffice.

One final introductory word: the patterns in this chapter apply to documents that are going to be printed, but they don't necessarily apply to on-line documentation. We'll have a discussion about what READER-FRIENDLY MEDIA are in Chapter 4, which raises the issue of print vs. on-line document delivery. Some guidelines for setting up on-line documents are given there.

Text on 50% of a Page

Problem   **How much space on a page should be devoted to text?**

Forces   The page layout should be aesthetic if it is to be pleasing to readers. The aesthetics of the page geometry are largely influenced by the size of the so-called 'live area' – the area in which the main text is placed, excluding headers or footers. The live area of a page is surrounded by the margins. Almost all readers prefer pages with ample margins to pages that appear to be crowded with text (West 1990).

Margins are not necessary for aesthetic reasons alone, but also for functional reasons. The inner margin (also called the 'gutter') must allow enough space for binding. All margins must allow enough space for readers to hold a page without obscuring any text (West 1990).

However, margins that are excessively large aren't appropriate either. Printing a document would require more paper than necessary, which is undesirable for economical as well as ecological reasons.

Apart from the size of the live area, its position influences a document's legibility. The optical centre of a page is the place where the reader's eye first focuses. The optical centre is slightly above the geometric centre of the page. The live area should therefore be slightly closer to the top than to the bottom of a page. In other words, the optimum margin size is smaller for the top margin than for the bottom margin (Conover 1985, West 1990).

Solution

About 50% of the page should be devoted to text.

The rest of the page is reserved for white space, headers and footers. This is a generally accepted rule among layout experts (Conover 1985, Tinker 1963, West 1990).

To put the centre of the text near the optical centre, the text should be positioned nearer to the top than to the bottom of the page. A ratio of 2:3:4:5 between the sizes of the inner, top, outer and bottom margins is often recommended as it allows the margin size to increase from inner to top to outer to bottom (Gulbins Kahrmann 1992).

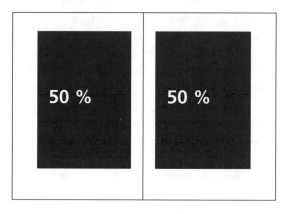

Figure 27. 50% text on a page

Some documents don't differentiate between left pages and right pages, so that the left and right margins are the same size. In this case, the margin ratio can be adjusted to, for example, 3:3:3:5. The bottom margin should still be larger than the top margin, however.

To obtain a pleasing page geometry, you should also take the following into account:

- Because headers and footers are not part of the live area of a page, they don't count when the 50% rule is implemented.

- The minimum gutter margin should be 2 cm, to allow for binding.

- A live area covering slightly more than 50% of the page is acceptable when not all of the live area is actually covered by text, for example due to the use of side-heads that leave enough white space.[6]

A standard A4 page has a size of 21 × 29.7 cm. Here margins of 2, 3, 4 and 5 cm meet the rule, leaving a live area of 15 × 21.7 cm. The live area space is 325.5 square cm, which is 52% of the A4 page.

Similar margin sizes can be used for the US letter format (size 21.59 × 27.94 cm), which yields a live area of approximately 15.6 × 20 cm – an area of 312 square cm (52% of the US letter page).

Discussion   The 50% rule is surprising to many people at first. When people look at a printed page, they often overestimate the amount of space devoted to the live area and underestimate the amount of space devoted to margins. Average readers estimate that the live area covers about 75% of a page, when it in fact covers only 50% (Tinker 1963). In other words, 50% text is more than it seems.

There is a limit on the line width that states that there should be about TWO ALPHABETS PER LINE, as shown in Figure 28. If more than two and a half lower-case alphabets fit on one line, the line is too wide. Once you have defined the live area of your page, you should check whether a line across it meets this rule, and otherwise employ techniques to reduce the line width. Having two columns per page is one option, using side-heads is another, using a larger font size is a third.

To give the live area a regular appearance and even texture, normally no more than TWO TYPEFACES should be used, and lines should be separated by 120% LINE SPACING.

Two Alphabets per Line

Problem   **What is the optimum line width?**

Forces   When reading, the reader's eyes travel along the line from left to right.[7] The eyes make small, jerky movements called 'saccades', between which there are periods called 'fixations'. Fixations last for about a quarter of a second, while

---

6. Side-heads are headings that are placed to the left or to the right of the actual paragraphs, as is done in this book for the second-level headings.

saccades are only 0.01 seconds long. It is during the fixations that information is picked up (Crowder 1982).

A line break interrupts the eye movement along the line. The reader's eyes have to shift back to the beginning of the next line. Short lines increase the number of line breaks. If lines are too short, the reader's eyes have to find the beginning of the next line more often than necessary, which breaks the flow of reading and makes reading tiresome (Conover 1985, Gulbins Kahrmann 1992).

On the other hand, lines that are too long also make reading difficult and tiresome. Long lines make it difficult for the reader's eyes to follow a line and to find the beginning of the next line once a line break occurs (Conover 1985, Gulbins Kahrmann 1992).

Moreover, the optimum line width depends on the typeface and type size used. Type set in larger sizes requires longer line widths (Conover 1985, Gulbins Kahrmann 1992).

Solution   **Approximately two lowercase alphabets of the standard typeface should fit on one line.**

As a rule of thumb, the lower limit is near one and a half lowercase alphabets, while the upper limit lies near two and a half and at most three lowercase alphabets (Gulbins Kahrmann 1992).

abcdefghijklmnopqrstuvwxyz abcdefghijklmnopqrstuvwxyz

Figure 28. Two alphabets per line

7. Some languages are not written from left to right, but, for example, from top to bottom. This pattern and the next do not apply to documents written in such languages.

If lines are too long, there are several ways to fix this problem:

- You can choose a larger type size.

- You can make the lines shorter by increasing the margins.

- You can make the lines shorter by using two columns rather than one.

- You can make the lines shorter by using side-heads.

Discussion When you choose to optimise the line width, either by increasing the margins or by using two columns, you should make sure that the page layout conforms to the TEXT ON 50% OF A PAGE rule.

Justified text can be problematic when the line width is near the lower limit. Since justification requires that the spacing between words (and sometimes between characters) be varied, unnaturally long word separations can occur. It is therefore important to use hyphenation (West 1990). Using ragged right rather than justification can also be worth considering.

There is also a subtle effect that spacing has on the range of acceptable line widths. When the standard of 120% LINE SPACING is slightly increased, line widths a little above two and a half lowercase alphabets can be acceptable.

120% Line Spacing

Problem **What is the optimum line spacing?**

Forces An even texture is crucial for the legibility of a document (West 1990). Reasonable spacing between words and lines is a prerequisite for an even texture. While word spacing is to a large degree determined by the typeface used, line spacing is not.

If there is too much line spacing, consecutive lines no longer form a unit – which they should – but instead appear to be separated from each other. This makes text difficult to read (West 1990).

Line spacing, however, should not be too small either. To explain why, we need to understand that the line spacing results from adding the type size to the 'leading' – the actual space between lines. A certain amount of leading is necessary to ensure that the ascenders of one line do not collide with the descenders of the previous line.[8]

Moreover, the appearance of a typeface is influenced by its x-height.[9] A typeface with a relatively small x-height appears to be smaller than its size suggests, and leaves more natural space between lines, thus reducing the need for extra leading.

Solution

The best line spacing is roughly 120% of the type size.

In other words, 20% leading is normally fine. For standard type sizes such as 10, 11 or 12 point this means that 2-point leading is appropriate.

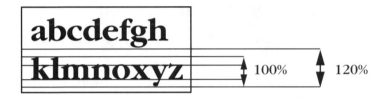

Figure 29. Line spacing

Fortunately, most word processors set the line spacing to about 120% as a default, and so provide you with the right spacing whatever type size you use.

In the following cases the spacing may need some fine-tuning:

* Spacing can be decreased for typefaces with a relatively small x-height.

* Spacing can be increased for typefaces with a relatively large x-height.

* Spacing should be increased for long lines.

Discussion

120% line spacing is appropriate for body text. Headings, however, are an exception, as they are supposed to make the structure of the text visible. To help readers perceive the structure of a text, headings should stand out not

---

8. An ascender is the letter stroke that extends above the x-height of a lowercase character; a descender is a stroke of a lowercase letter that extends below the x-height.

9. The x-height is the height of the lowercase letter 'x'.

only by an increased type size, but also by a line spacing that may exceed 120%.

The optimum line width is defined by the TWO ALPHABETS PER LINE pattern. You can, however, bend this rule a little. If you increase the spacing, lines that slightly increase the standard line width will still be acceptable. However, this technique can be applied only to a small extent. If lines contain significantly more than two and a half lowercase alphabets, they are inappropriate, even with increased spacing.

Two Typefaces

Problem   **How many typefaces are appropriate, and which?**

Forces   Word processors often offer a large variety of typefaces and type sizes to choose from whenever authors wish to express the different meanings text can have, such as headings, emphasis, references or citations.

However, when you look at a document that uses many different typefaces you'll notice that the document appears to be chaotic: using a large number of typefaces is problematic both for aesthetic and for ergonomic reasons.

Moreover, using many different typefaces is completely unnecessary, since things such as emphasis can very well be expressed with the type variations available.

But even if we restrict ourselves to using only a small number of typefaces, which ones should we use? Typefaces can express things such as soundness, formality, innovation, fashion and so on (Conover 1985). They should therefore be chosen in accordance with what they represent. Software project documents normally aren't supposed to express fashion or a 'trendy' style – the major requirement is that typefaces be highly legible.

To this end we need to distinguish between serif and sans-serif typefaces. Serifs are the short lines that cross the ends of the strokes of a printed letter. As far as body text is concerned, serif typefaces are more legible than sans-serif typefaces, and should therefore be given preference. However, single pieces of text printed in a sans-serif typeface stand out from the main text and can attract the reader's eye (Gulbins Kahrmann 1992).

Solution   **In most cases, two typefaces per document are appropriate – a serif typeface for the body text and a sans-serif typeface for the headings.**

You should also take the following into account:

- There is nothing completely wrong with using only one typeface throughout an entire document. In this case a serif typeface should be chosen for legibility reasons. However, a second typeface can improve a document's appearance.

- Using more than two typefaces is almost always inappropriate. A possible exception is the use of a third typeface for code fragments included in a document. The third typeface should still be used sparingly.

- The type size for body text should be 10 to 12 point, while 14 to 18 point is appropriate for headings, and up to 24 point for chapter and document titles.

Example

Here Frutiger (12 point) is the sans-serif typeface chosen for the heading. The body text is printed in Garamond (11 point), which is a serif typeface.

Example

Here Helvetica (12 point) is the sans-serif typeface chosen for the heading. The body text is printed in Times New Roman (11 point), another serif typeface.

Figure 30. Different typefaces

There is no general rule to tell you which typefaces you should use, this is matter of personal taste. The more traditional typefaces such as *Times* and *Garamond* tend to offer a higher legibility than more fashionable typefaces; therefore they seem more appropriate for the documentation of software projects.

When you choose different typefaces for body text and headings, these typefaces should not be too similar, so that they can easily be told apart. Still, they have to fit together in an aesthetic sense. Typical examples are *Times* and

Helvetica or *Garamond* and *Frutiger* (Gulbins Kahrmann 1992), as shown in Figure 30.

Discussion When this pattern speaks of 'body text', it means text in normal paragraphs as well as text used in tables or diagrams (except screen shots, whiteboard copies, etc.). There is no need to use different typefaces in tables or diagrams compared with the main text.

Neither is there a need to express emphasis through different typefaces. In fact, it's counter-intuitive. You can express all necessary kinds of emphasis by CAREFUL USE OF TYPE VARIATIONS.

Careful Use of Type Variations

Problem **How can parts of a text be emphasised?**

Forces You can use type variations to express emphasis, cross-references, etc. When used this way, different type variations help readers to understand the text, and in particular to understand the particular role that some words take on.

There is, however, a drawback to the use of type variations. Normal lower-case words appear in a characteristic shape defined by the ascenders and descenders of the letters. A characteristic shape is crucial for a word's legibility. Many type variations don't feature the characteristic shape as much as a standard lowercase typeface does, and therefore decrease the legibility.

Let's take a look at the different type variations in detail. Words printed in italics still have a characteristic shape. Nonetheless, italics slightly decrease the legibility of text. Reading text printed in italics takes about 4% more time than reading the same text printed in a standard lowercase type (Tinker 1963).

Capital letters do not feature a characteristic shape at all. They decrease the legibility of text quite dramatically. Reading text printed in all capital letters requires about 12% more time than a normal text (Tinker 1963). Moreover, 'all caps' are not appreciated by a vast majority of readers. In addition, all caps break the flow of a text.

The same is true for underlines. Underlines used to be a common technique on typewriters, where no other style elements were available. But both underlines and all capital letters are hardly ever used in printed books.

Solution

Type variations can be used for emphasis, but they should be used with care.

The following type variations are considered fine style elements (Conover 1985):

- Boldface can be used to emphasise single paragraphs.

- Italics are commonly used to place emphasis on a particular word.

- Small caps are often used to represent cross-references or people's names.[10]

All capital letters and underlines decrease the legibility to such an extent that they should be avoided altogether.

Figure 31. Shapes of different type styles

Discussion

You can use special font styles when you organise a document as STRUCTURED INFORMATION. For example, boldface is often used to let THUMBNAIL SKETCHES stand out from the remaining text. Italics and small caps can be useful for references to other documents.

Using underlines is fairly common for hyperlinks in on-line documents. This may be justified, but printed documents are a different matter. Since this chapter is about printed documents, however, underlines are not recommended.

---

10. In contrast to all caps, small caps clearly have a less bulky feel, so their occasional use is fine. In addition, small caps can be set with a leading capital, in which case they offer some characteristic shape.

Careful Ruling and Shading

Problem   **How can table cells be separated?**

Forces   Documents created in software projects often include tables. To easily access the information in a table, readers must be able to recognise the table cells at first glance. Moreover, the table's heading must be immediately clear.

There are various ways to achieve these goals: the use of white space, ruling and shading.

The use of white space between the table cells, however, is problematic, since quite a bit of white space is necessary if the separation of cells is to be clear, in particular when table cells extend over more than one line. If you use white space for separating table cells, you lose space that otherwise you could use for text.

Ruling is a more effective technique for separating table cells. However, ruling is fine only as long as the lines surrounding the table cells have the right thickness. Lines that are too thin are difficult to recognise, while lines that are too thick aren't aesthetically pleasing and irritate the reader. Ideally, lines separating table cells should have about the same thickness as the letters of the typeface chosen for body text.

Finally, shading can provide structure to a table, but must not lead to a poor contrast between the text and its background.

Solution   **Careful ruling and shading leads to highly legible tables.**

Technically, careful ruling and shading means the following:

- Lines surrounding table cells have the right thickness if they are about as thick as the uppercase letter I (Gulbins Kahrmann 1992).

- Greyscales ranging from 10% to 20% guarantee good contrast and high legibility.

You can combine both techniques, for example by using ruling to separate table cells and shading to identify the table heading.

Task	Deadline
Work package 1	2003-Jul-20
Work package 2	2003-Aug-31
Work package 3	2003-Sep-10
Work package 4	2003-Oct-15

Figure 32. Table ruling and shading

Discussion   Obviously, careful ruling and shading is useful in order to achieve UNAMBIG-UOUS TABLES, but is in fact applicable to the presentation of STRUCTURED INFORMATION in general.

The CAREFUL USE OF TYPE VARIATIONS can complement ruling and shading, for example through the use of boldface in the table heading.

Adjacent Placement

Problem   **How can tables and diagrams be integrated into text?**

Forces   The placement of tables and diagrams can be difficult. The ideal place for a table or diagram is directly below the line where it is referenced, as this is where the reader first looks for it. However, the larger a table or diagram is, the smaller is the chance that it will fit in the ideal place. There might not be enough room left on the page.

As far as tables are concerned, the problem can be solved by allowing page breaks to be inserted within a table. This, however, does not work for diagrams.

The obvious idea is to insert a page break between the paragraph and the diagram if the diagram doesn't fit on the current page, which causes the diagram to appear on the next page. This strategy, however, is fine only if no large empty space occurs at the bottom of the current page.

Sometimes, however, a large empty space does occur. Especially large diagrams can cause half-empty pages, which is clearly undesirable. In such a case, we need to decouple the diagram from the paragraph in which it is referenced and to which it would normally be anchored. We may need to place the diagram anywhere near the paragraph, perhaps below, perhaps above, perhaps on the next page.

The consequence is that the paragraph does not immediately precede the diagram and other text appears in between. This is acceptable, but requires that all diagrams be numbered and be referred to by their numbers, rather than by an expression like 'the following diagram'. The same applies to tables if page breaks within tables are to be avoided.

Even the strategy of decoupling large diagrams or tables from the referencing text might not be sufficient. If a document contains a large number of diagrams, there might not be enough text to fill the gaps left by the diagrams.

Solution **Diagrams and tables are best placed close to the text from which they are referenced.**

The following techniques can help you to put tables and diagrams as near to the referencing paragraph as possible without creating awkward empty spaces on the page:

- Small tables and diagrams can often be integrated into the text flow, and appear directly below the paragraph in which they are referenced.

- Larger diagrams must be allowed to 'float', that is, they must be required to appear anywhere near the paragraph from where they are referenced, but not necessarily directly below that paragraph. Text is allowed to fill the gaps.

- Larger tables, from 4 rows onwards, should allow for page breaks.

- Diagrams must be given numbers and must be referred to by their numbers.

- If there are too many diagrams for smooth integration into the text flow, moving at least some of them into an appendix can be preferable, as this may allow the text flow to remain intact. (Half-empty pages are much more acceptable in an appendix than in the main text.)

Discussion Most word processors allow the use of anchored frames in which a diagram can be placed. Such an anchored frame is automatically moved with the paragraph to which it is anchored. Good systems also allow anchored frames to be defined as floating, which means that a frame is kept near the paragraph, but may be placed on the next page if this allows better text flow on the current page. If it is available, choose this option for large diagrams.

Allowing page breaks in tables makes the placement of tables easier. Still, page breaks in tables should only be allowed as long as they don't sacrifice COHERENT PAGES.

Coherent Pages

Problem   **What options exist to avoid awkward pagination that tears related information apart?**

Forces   Page breaks are a perfectly normal thing, yet some page breaks seem to be acceptable, while others don't. Page breaks are particularly awkward when they break the flow unnecessarily and force readers to jump back and forth.

This is the case whenever a page break makes a small snippet of information appear on one page and related material appear on the next or the previous page. One example is a section heading that appears on the bottom of a page while the first paragraph of that section appears on the next page. Others are 'widow' or 'orphan' lines. A widow is the last line of a paragraph that appears isolated at the top of a page, while an orphan is the first line of a paragraph that appears isolated at the bottom of a page.

Such page breaks are irritating and can make it difficult for readers to grasp an idea or line of argument, especially for readers who browse a document quickly.

Solution   **The reading flow is supported by coherent pages – pages that make sure a minimum of related information appears on either side of a page break.**

You can achieve coherent pages by using the following rules:

- No headings should appear at the bottom of a page. A heading is always followed by at least one paragraph that appears on the same page.

- There are no widow or orphan lines. At least two lines of a paragraph must be kept together on each page.

- Small tables should appear on one page. If a page break must occur within a table, the widow line rule applies: at least two table rows must be kept together on each page.

- There are no page breaks within table cells.

Discussion   All these rules can be implemented with standard word processors fairly easily. You need to disallow widow and orphan lines for all paragraph types and to force all paragraph types for headings to be kept with any paragraph that follows. You also have to disallow page breaks for the paragraph types used in table cells – which of course requires that distinct paragraph types be used in table cells. Only the page breaks within tables (as opposed to within table cells) might require manual intervention.

Coherent pages can take on a slightly different form in the context of STRUCTURED INFORMATION. You can decide not to allow page breaks within building blocks. If you look back at Figure 12 on page 69, you see a page that consists of a heading and four blocks. Such a structure profits from not being interrupted by page breaks. However, if the building blocks become large, you must allow page breaks, otherwise half-empty pages would be the consequence – a contradiction to having TEXT ON 50% OF A PAGE.

Experience Reports

There are myriads of examples of the typographical patterns described in this chapter. You can find instances of these patterns in almost every printed book – the patterns are common practice. If you're interested in seeing a large variety of applications of these patterns, a look at a couple of printed books will do.

The following figures, however, show that the patterns can also be used in project documentation easily. Figure 33 shows the page we already know from the beginning of this chapter, taken from the usage concept of Project Persistor. Figure 34 shows a page from the requirements document of Project Contentis. Annotations point out where the patterns have been applied, and how.[11]

---

11. Don't be surprised by the relatively small font in these examples. The original documents were A4 and had to be shrunk to fit the page size of this book. The original font did allow for comfortable reading.

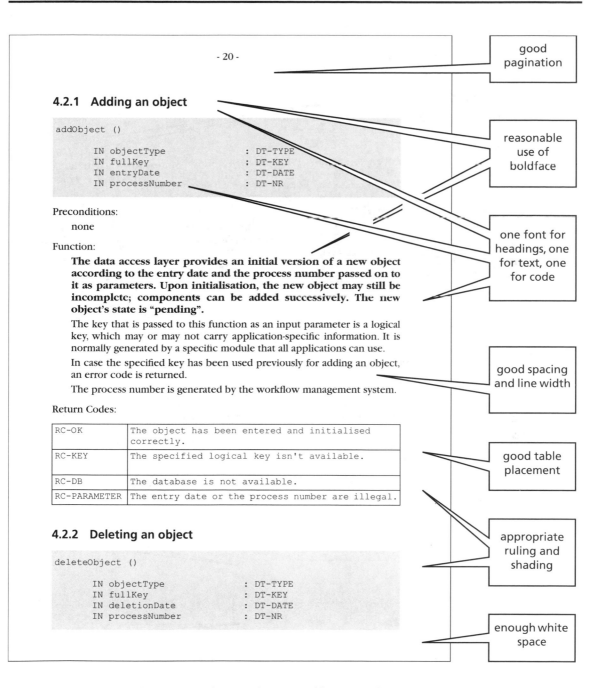

- 20 -

4.2.1 Adding an object

```
addObject ()

        IN objectType         : DT-TYPE
        IN fullKey            : DT-KEY
        IN entryDate          : DT-DATE
        IN processNumber      : DT-NR
```

Preconditions:

Function:

The data access layer provides an initial version of a new object according to the entry date and the process number passed on to it as parameters. Upon initialisation, the new object may still be incomplete; components can be added successively. The new object's state is "pending".

The key that is passed to this function as an input parameter is a logical key, which may or may not carry application-specific information. It is normally generated by a specific module that all applications can use.

In case the specified key has been used previously for adding an object, an error code is returned.

The process number is generated by the workflow management system.

Return Codes:

RC-OK	The object has been entered and initialised correctly.
RC-KEY	The specified logical key isn't available.
RC-DB	The database is not available.
RC-PARAMETER	The entry date or the process number are illegal.

4.2.2 Deleting an object

```
deleteObject ()

        IN objectType         : DT-TYPE
        IN fullKey            : DT-KEY
        IN deletionDate       : DT-DATE
        IN processNumber      : DT-NR
```

good pagination

reasonable use of boldface

one font for headings, one for text, one for code

good spacing and line width

good table placement

appropriate ruling and shading

enough white space

Figure 33. Project Persistor: good layout and typography

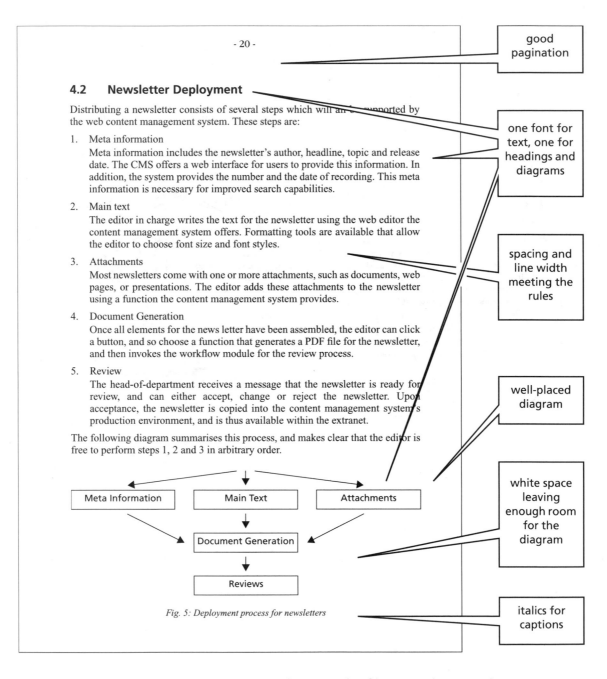

4.2   Newsletter Deployment

- 20 -

good pagination

Distributing a newsletter consists of several steps which will an supported by the web content management system. These steps are:

one font for text, one for headings and diagrams

1. Meta information
    Meta information includes the newsletter's author, headline, topic and release date. The CMS offers a web interface for users to provide this information. In addition, the system provides the number and the date of recording. This meta information is necessary for improved search capabilities.

2. Main text
    The editor in charge writes the text for the newsletter using the web editor the content management system offers. Formatting tools are available that allow the editor to choose font size and font styles.

spacing and line width meeting the rules

3. Attachments
    Most newsletters come with one or more attachments, such as documents, web pages, or presentations. The editor adds these attachments to the newsletter using a function the content management system provides.

4. Document Generation
    Once all elements for the news letter have been assembled, the editor can click a button, and so choose a function that generates a PDF file for the newsletter, and then invokes the workflow module for the review process.

5. Review
    The head-of-department receives a message that the newsletter is ready for review, and can either accept, change or reject the newsletter. Upon acceptance, the newsletter is copied into the content management system's production environment, and is thus available within the extranet.

well-placed diagram

The following diagram summarises this process, and makes clear that the editor is free to perform steps 1, 2 and 3 in arbitrary order.

white space leaving enough room for the diagram

| Meta Information | Main Text | Attachments |

| Document Generation |

| Reviews |

Fig. 5: Deployment process for newsletters

italics for captions

Figure 34. Project Contentis: another example of layout and typography

Although all example documents feature almost all patterns from this chapter, they do not have the same layout. You can see that the typographical patterns presented leave ample room for creativity – or for following layout guidelines that hold for an organisation or a project. The patterns provide a framework for increasing the legibility and the aesthetics of printed documents, but they leave a lot of their implementation open. You can apply the typographical patterns in many different and creative ways.

4 Infrastructure and Technical Organisation

Managing documentation and managing software is essentially the same thing.

Anonymous

So far this book has dealt with the documents that we need in our software projects and what they should look like. We have talked about their contents, their structure and their layout. This chapter looks at the tools and techniques that we can use to obtain such documents and to make them available to a project team. Among other things, documents have to be processed and printed, stored and retrieved.

To summarise, this chapter brings up the issue of what the documentation infrastructure should look like and how it can be organised.

I'd like to begin with an example that demonstrates why organising the documentation infrastructure is necessary. Look at the file system structure illustrated in Figure 35, which I found in a project a while ago.

In this project, nobody was able to find the documents they were looking for. The directories overlap, related documents don't seem to be grouped into directories, copies of documents have been scattered over different directories, and symbolic links complete the confusion. It's a complete mess – and Figure 35 shows just an excerpt. Yet this is a scenario I found in a real-world project.

Team members in this project put the documents they had written more or less anywhere. More than once someone assumed a document did not exist, when in fact it was just hidden in the chaos. Redundant versions of docu-

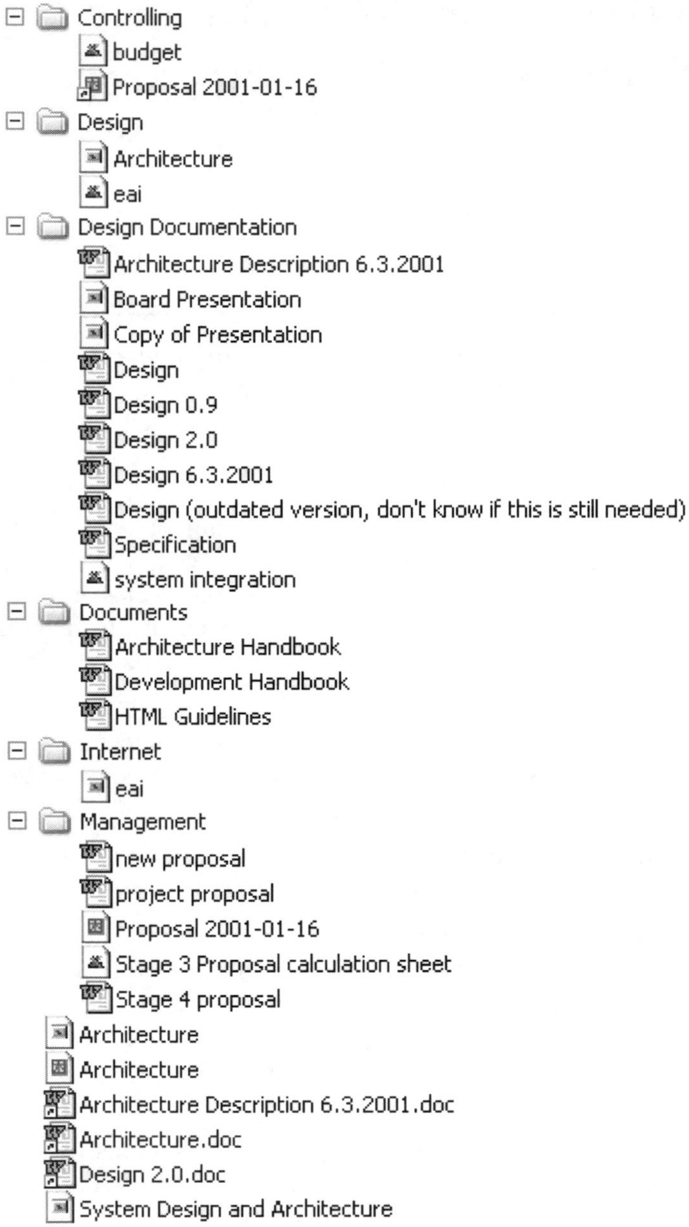

- Controlling
  - budget
  - Proposal 2001-01-16
- Design
  - Architecture
  - eai
- Design Documentation
  - Architecture Description 6.3.2001
  - Board Presentation
  - Copy of Presentation
  - Design
  - Design 0.9
  - Design 2.0
  - Design 6.3.2001
  - Design (outdated version, don't know if this is still needed)
  - Specification
  - system integration
- Documents
  - Architecture Handbook
  - Development Handbook
  - HTML Guidelines
- Internet
  - eai
- Management
  - new proposal
  - project proposal
  - Proposal 2001-01-16
  - Stage 3 Proposal calculation sheet
  - Stage 4 proposal
- Architecture
- Architecture
- Architecture Description 6.3.2001.doc
- Architecture.doc
- Design 2.0.doc
- System Design and Architecture

Figure 35. Poorly organised project documentation

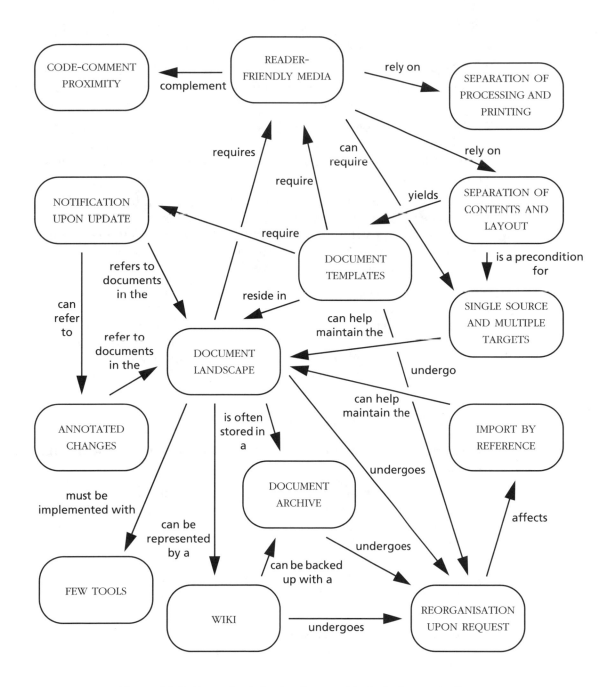

Figure 36. Patterns for infrastructure and technical organisation

ments were kept, inconsistencies occurred and outdated versions were the source of much confusion.

We certainly want to avoid a scenario like this, and I think it's clear from this example that a little organisation is necessary. But how much organisation do we need? After all, over-organisation is the opposite of an agile approach.

A follow-up question deals with tools. To which extent are tools helpful as far as producing and maintaining the documentation is concerned? There is much value in tools if they make our jobs easier, but an over-emphasis on tools isn't agile either.

These questions demarcate the area that the patterns in this chapter address. The patterns deal with the technical organisation of all the documents produced in a project, from just a handful of short papers to the comprehensive documentation found in larger projects or projects with a higher criticality. Figure 36 gives an overview.

The patterns cannot provide prefabricated solutions to all problems associated with the technical organisation of project documents – project documentation can take on too many different forms for off-the-shelf solutions to be possible. Instead, these patterns describe the principles that underlie an agile approach to the creation and the maintenance of project documents and the management of the relationships between them.

Document Landscape

Problem

How can team members get a good overview of what documentation exists in a project?

Forces

Documentation, when it is poorly organised, will ultimately fail to serve its overall purpose of making project expertise available to other team members and to future projects. There's no point in producing documents if potential readers don't know that they exist. On a more technical level, organising project documentation must serve two purposes: authors among the team members must be told how to integrate new documents into the existing documentation, and readers must be told where to look for specific documents.

What does such an organisation look like? To this end, it is helpful to remember that project documents are often connected by various kinds of relationships, and to examine how humans organise related items in their minds.

Cognitive psychology tells us that humans can represent sets of related items as mental images, or landscapes in our minds. In his book *How The Mind Works*, Steven Pinker explains that the human brain is well trained to recognise objects by their shapes, and that complex objects create a reference frame by which their parts can be located (Pinker 1997).

This suggests that a good way to represent the set of documents is some kind of landscape – but which? We will not only *imagine* this landscape, but when we browse the documentation, we will, in a way, *navigate* through it. Let's therefore take a look at hypertexts.

Experiences with hypertexts suggest that linked networks are relatively easy to follow if they span a tree (Botafogo Rivlin Shneiderman 1992) – a tree represents a balance between structure and comprehensibility. Apparently most users prefer a broad tree to a narrow one: in most cases, a depth of 3 is sufficient (Horton 1994). Some studies suggest that hypertexts need not be exact trees, as short-cuts or multiple entry points seem to be fine (Furnas Zacks 1994).

Solution

The project documentation can be represented as a kind of landscape that team members can use as a mental map when they retrieve or add information. A document landscape that roughly forms a tree suits human intuition best.

Ideally, the document landscape follows the project structure. Figure 37 shows an example. Documents are grouped if they are closely related. This landscape presents an intuitive way of representing the project documentation. It isn't static, though, but evolves as the project goes on.

There are various ways in which you can implement a document landscape:

- The easiest way is to use file system directories and subdirectories. Associating directories with topics leads to an easy but efficient organisation, as long as there are no overlaps caused by orthogonal topics.

- In addition, you can use a diagram that visualises the document landscape (like the one in Figure 37) and include that diagram into an introductory document. Such a document describes the project and explains what other documents exist, their purpose and how they can be obtained.

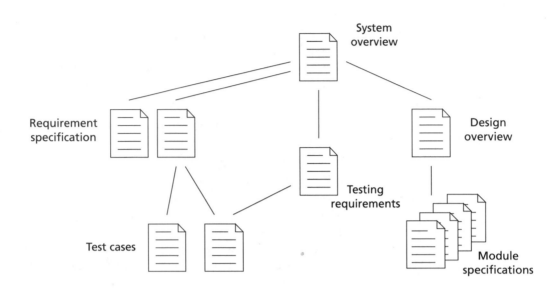

Figure 37. A document landscape

- You can put the document landscape on-line with hyperlinks acting as pathways to the actual documents, allowing users to actually travel through the document landscape.

Discussion   Which technique should be preferred? Lurking behind this question is the desire to use READER-FRIENDLY MEDIA when presenting information. Due to its high degree of referentiality, the document landscape is often best presented on-line. If you give all team members read and write access, the document landscape amounts to a project WIKI. Whether an on-line presentation is the medium of choice ultimately depends on the typical scenario in which the TARGET READERS will use the document landscape. A crucial question to ask here is whether all members of the project team have access to an intranet by which they can obtain the individual documents.

If the document landscape is indeed put on-line, should it be enhanced with a search engine? In large projects this can be worth considering. The usefulness of a search engine is generally limited, though, since search engines suffer from a trade-off between recall and precision. Recall and precision typically add up to 100 percent (Salton 1989)[12]: 50 percent recall and 50 percent precision can be considered a typical result (Dumais 1988). Nevertheless, a search engine can prove useful if a large number of documents have to be managed and the overview given by the document landscape, however useful, isn't fully sufficient.

You can sense the importance of this pattern by an analogy to individual documents. We have seen that the GUIDELINES FOR READERS serve as a road map to an individual document, and similarly a document landscape provides a way to approach the documentation of an entire project.

Finally, the document landscape's degree of cohesion gives you feedback on how well the project documentation meets the goal of presenting FOCUSED INFORMATION. If it turns out to be difficult to find an appropriate structure for the document landscape, a lack of focus in the individual documents may be the cause, possibly giving rise to a reorganisation of the project documentation.

Document Archive

Problem

How can projects avoid the loss of any document versions?

Forces

Project documents are typically organised in a system of folders and sub-folders, hopefully in a well-defined way so that readers are able to retrieve a particular document quickly.

However, many documents undergo change as a project goes on. It can become necessary to track down information in an older version of a document. Therefore it sometimes isn't sufficient to keep only the most recent versions of all documents.

Still, users often prefer not to see the old versions of all documents, but to have the old versions hidden and deal with them only when they really need to do so.

---

12. *Recall* describes how much of the relevant information is found, while *precision* describes how much of the information found is relevant. If a search yields 80% of all relevant information, then only about 20% of the results are relevant – the other results have just slipped in due to a lack of precision. If you restrict the search parameters so that 80% of the results are relevant, the recall typically goes down to about 20% – the remaining 80% of relevant results are not found.

Moreover, as we keep different versions of documents, we need to make sure that we don't confuse them. Sometimes several people contribute to a document, so we need a mechanism that prevents these people from working on the same version at the same time, overriding each other's work.

Finally, we must keep in mind that technical problems such as hard disk crashes can lead to project documentation being lost. This sounds trivial, but much damage has been done, ruining the work of weeks or months, by a single hardware failure.

Solution

Archiving project documentation offers the advantage that versions can be retrieved when necessary.

A document archive[13] can have different degrees of sophistication.

- The simplest form of archiving consists of a naming convention for old document versions, which are not deleted, but remain in the file system, along with a central back-up service that covers the entire project documentation.

- A configuration management system offers more features. It allows users to check in and check out documents. A locking mechanism makes sure that changes to a document can be made only by the person who has checked it out. The system stores old versions automatically and retrieves them on request (Berczuk Appelton 2003).

As we intend to use the simplest tools that fulfil our purposes, the idea of file-system based versioning has great appeal, as it doesn't require any extra tools, despite the fact that it doesn't render old versions invisible.

However, many projects use a configuration management system anyway, especially for source code. In this case, the second option does not represent additional effort and is well worth considering. A fairly simple configuration management system is usually appropriate, because complex systems require a learning effort that is rarely justified.

Discussion

Setting up a DOCUMENT LANDSCAPE establishes a tree-like structure. An archive is one way to implement such a landscape. You can group related documents

---

13. An *archive* here refers to any mechanism used to keep track of versions. Unlike a more narrow meaning of the term, archiving does not necessarily imply that old versions be moved to off-line storage media for purposes such as freeing up space.

in folders and possibly sub-folders, either in the file system or in a configuration management system.

Wiki

Problem   **How can documentation be given a more interactive edge?**

Forces   Documentation has much in its favour, long-term and wide availability among other things. However, interaction is important in a collaborative team. People have questions, or would like to give answers. It's been said many times before: documentation and interaction aren't opposed to each other, but complement each other.

For example, you might have a question concerning a document while its author is on leave. Perhaps someone else also knows the answer, but you don't know who that person might be.

To this end, technical support for the combination of documentation and interaction could be helpful. What might support look like? It should aim to increase interaction among the team, but should also take into account that asynchronous communication might be required.

Solution   **A Wiki offers access to the project documentation via an intranet server, and in addition allows the team to post notes and messages to others as necessary.**

A Wiki is essentially a Web site to which all team members have both read and write access.[14]

As a team member, you can use a Wiki in various ways:

- You can add documents or new versions of documents.

- You can download the documents you need.

- You can leave messages for others with any new ideas or questions you might have.

- You can answer messages from others.

---

14. 'Wiki' is the Hawaiian word for 'quick'. The term 'Wiki Web' was introduced by Ward Cunningham for collaborative Web sites that give their users quick read and write access (Leuf Cunningham 2001).

In other words, a Wiki is a forum for collaborative interactive yet asynchronous communication.

Discussion   A Wiki implements the project's DOCUMENT LANDSCAPE and allows the team members to navigate through it. A Wiki doesn't provide the safety with respect to versioning that a DOCUMENT ARCHIVE does. However, you can install an archive at the Wiki's back-end to take care of things such as versioning and back-up.

Wikis are well known for not imposing any write-access restrictions on their users: everybody can change anything. This may seem a bit risky when a large and anonymous group of people have access, although experiences are positive, and to be on the safe side, you can still make back-ups. A project team, however, isn't an anonymous mass, and general access for everybody shouldn't represent a problem. Nevertheless, most project documents have ONE RESPONSIBLE AUTHOR, and team members can be asked to check with the person who is in charge of a document before they make changes to it.

Because a project Wiki offers a higher degree of interaction than a mere archive does, establishing a Wiki gets you on your way towards an INFORMATION MARKETPLACE in which documents are actively offered and exchanged.

Code-Comment Proximity

Problem   **What is an easy way to maintain documentation that refers to the actual code?**

Forces   Documentation can take on different forms. First, documentation consists of the documents that are produced in a project. Second, documentation covers the comments that programmers put into the source code, which are not to be ignored. The question here is, which form of documentation should we prefer?

A certain proximity of code and the comments that refer to it offers several advantages. First, programmers, when they look at a program, don't have to search for helpful commentary elsewhere.

Second, source code comments are relatively easy to maintain. If you change something in a program and its documentation is located somewhere else, the chances are that you will forget to change the documentation accordingly.

Updates are much easier if all you need to do is to update a few comments in the code.

Literate Programming goes one step further. Literate programming denotes a programming style that was put forward by Donald Knuth. He suggested that programs should be written in a way that explains to other humans what the computer is supposed to do (Knuth 1992). The careful choice of variable names is particularly important. Ideally, a program turns into a text that needs no further comments.

But is this always possible? Not every topic that requires documentation is directly related to the code. There are higher-level topics such as user requirements or the software architecture that cannot be related to single lines of code, and which are therefore beyond what can be documented within a program.

Solution

Documentation of the code, to the extent that a project team considers it necessary, is best done through source code comments. Separate documents should be reserved for higher-level issues such as overviews, requirements, design and architecture.

The following guidelines will help to make code comments as simple as possible.

- Keep the software as clear as possible, for example through well-chosen names for objects and functions.

- Add comments only when the code alone doesn't provide enough information, and keep those comments close to the code to which they refer.

The proximity of code and the corresponding comments makes the comments relatively easy to maintain. Whenever you change the code, you have the corresponding comments right in front of you and you can change them accordingly. Updates to documents will only be necessary when changes affect more than just the code, such as the overall design.

Discussion

This pattern already touches the subject of READER-FRIENDLY MEDIA. That pattern focuses on the question of the choice of media for project documents, but that question is reasonable only if we are certain that a document is the right medium at all. The current pattern points out that for some information a document may not be necessary, and that the information is better kept within the program.

Reader-Friendly Media

Problem   **Which is more appropriate: documents intended for on-line use, or documents intended for print?**

Forces   For ergonomic reasons, most people prefer to read paper documents rather than on-line documents. This is true in particular for longer documents which readers may spend more time reading. Printed documents offer better resolution and contrast than a computer screen, printed documents don't need an electrical power supply, and readers can take printed documents with them without having to carry a computer around (Hsu Mitchell 1997). Printed documents can easily be marked for making editorial comments. To summarise, paper allows readers to sit down, lie back and concentrate.

There is an on-going discussion about whether printed documents and books will eventually be replaced by electronic versions. There are technological advances as far as the ergonomics of electronic documents are concerned (Press 2000). But for the time being, most people prefer printed documents for reading.

However, some project documents are characterised by a high degree of referentiality. There can be cross-references within documents, as well as references to other documents. Only electronic documents offer mechanisms such as hyperlinks that make navigation of such references easy. Readers have to use on-line documents if they wish to use such features (Hsu Mitchell 1997).

Moreover, on-line presentations can allow readers to play a more active role. In an advanced scenario, readers can become involved if the documentation includes a simulation or an animation, though this is fairly uncommon for the documentation of normal software projects.

There are two more arguments that seem to suggest an advantage that on-line documents have over printed documents. Neither argument holds, but both should be mentioned for clarity's sake.

First, it may sound interesting to present quickly-changing documents on-line, in the hope that readers automatically read the most recent versions. It's a nice idea – but it doesn't work. When people find that they have to read such a document, they frequently print it, even if wasn't meant for printing in the first place, and so won't notice when there is an update available on-line.

Second, the use of search engines is sometimes used as an argument for electronic documents, but this isn't a valid argument either. Applying a search engine to a document requires that the document be available electronically, yet it has nothing to do with the medium at which the document is targeted: documents that are going to be printed can be parsed just as well as on-line documents can.

Solution

The choice of a medium must reflect a document's typical usage. The rule of thumb is: print is good for reading, on-line is good for looking things up.

The following guidelines can help you make the decision.

- Some documents will typically be read, as opposed to being browsed, at least in parts. Team members will sit down and concentrate on the parts in which they are interested. Perhaps they'll take the document home or on a business trip. These documents should be provided in a format that allows printing.

- Some documents are used in a way that cannot really be referred to as 'reading'. Rather, people take a brief look at such documents, or browse through them, often during programming or design, typically spending only a short period of time on them. Such documents are best presented on-line.

The following table summarises which medium is typically best suited for several kinds of documents.

Print	On-line
Feasibility study	Document landscape
Concept or strategy paper	Architectural overview
Architectural overview	API description
Specification	User manual
Design document	On-line help
Usage concept	On-line simulation
Management summary	Glossary
Glossary	

As the table shows, there is no clear separation between those documents that are best presented as print and those that are best presented on line. The architectural overview is listed under both print and on-line, as is the glossary.

So what is ultimately the 'right' medium? The truth is that there are documents that some readers prefer to print that others prefer to use on line, and all have reasons for their choice. This happens with documents that some readers will read from beginning to end, but that others use for looking up information and for following references. In this case meeting readers' needs requires that you provide *both* a printable version and an on-line version.

Discussion   If a document is necessary both on paper and on-line, it is sometimes tempting to set up the document for on-line use and use the same version for printing. Besides the reduction in effort, this has the advantage that information isn't kept redundantly in two documents. Nevertheless, this isn't a good idea. Documents that aren't properly formatted don't print very well. Using on-line documents for printing should be avoided for ergonomic reasons. It is a much better idea to generate the on-line version automatically – a feature that many word processors offer, and one that avoids redundancy.

Generating on-line documents automatically isn't only useful when we require both a print an on-line version. Typical on-line documents – those we don't read, but just browse through, those with many references – can often be extracted from other sources. For example, an API description can often be obtained from source code comments. Generating on-line documents is a good idea whenever possible, as it avoids inconsistencies by keeping a SINGLE SOURCE AND MULTIPLE TARGETS.

The decision over media typically isn't restricted to individual documents, but extends to all documents of a particular kind, at least within a project. You decide on the medium for all specifications, for example, rather than for just one specification. The decision therefore strongly influences the definition of DOCUMENT TEMPLATES that form the basis for several documents of the same kind.

Different media place different requirements on layout and formatting. Documents that are going to be printed should follow the guidelines presented in Chapter 3 on *Layout and Typography*. These guidelines, however, do not necessarily apply to on-line documents.

As far as on-line documentation is concerned, the guidelines to follow are essentially those given in the literature for organising Web sites. Since this book has its main focus on printed documents, such guidelines are beyond its scope, but the literature offers plenty of sources. One example is Jakob Nielsen's book on *Designing Web Usability* (Nielsen 2000), another is William Horton's book on *Designing and Writing Online Documentation* (Horton 1994). On-line documentation is also subject to patterns: Robert Orenstein has published a *Pattern Language for an Essay-Based Web Site* (Orenstein 1996). Among other things, he recommends *Low-depth Document Trees* and an *Introductory Section* with an *Introductory Picture*.

Separation of Contents and Layout

Problem   **How can the layouts of text documents be changed and reused easily?**

Forces   The layout of a document may have to change. First, we may have to adapt the layout to conform to some standard, perhaps following specific guidelines, perhaps following a customer's request. Second, and more likely, we may have to support an additional output channel: perhaps a print document must be made available for on-line use as well.

Going through all the paragraphs of a document just to change its appearance is a tedious job, and an unacceptable one. We have to perform such a change at the least possible cost. Whether we perform the layout change manually, or whether a tool is available, changes to the layout must not turn out to be cost-intensive activities.

Moreover, once a good layout has been designed, we want to be able to reuse it for other documents as well. How could we do that?

If we take a look at content management systems, we can see what a possible solution might look like. Content management systems decouple contents and layout: they record the contents without formatting on one hand, and on the other provide mechanisms to define layout styles. The degree of sophistication found in content management systems is unnecessary for ordinary project documents, but the underlying principle hints at a direction we can take.

Solution   **Layout styles can be defined and assigned to content portions. These layout styles can easily be changed and can be reused across documents.**

Using a typical word processor, the separation of content and layout can be implemented very easily in the following way:

- Define the necessary paragraph types for your document.

- Assign a format to each paragraph type.

- Assign a paragraph type to each paragraph, and so determine that paragraph's layout.

- Avoid any overrides of the format that a paragraph has been assigned by its type.

This implementation is illustrated in Figure 38.

Another option, though a less common one, is to use XML to structure the contents of a document, and to use XSLT to assign formats to the individual XML blocks. Or you could write documents in HTML, and provide the formatting through style sheets (CSS).

In either case, changing the definition of the layout affects the entire document consistently, wherever the particular layout style is used. Reusing the layout styles in other documents is not a problem either.

Discussion   This pattern is the precondition for two other patterns. First, without a separation of contents and layout, DOCUMENT TEMPLATES would not be possible. Such templates define content-independent formatting that is reused in all the documents that are derived from them.

Second, we can sometimes generate documents automatically, which gives us a SINGLE SOURCE AND MULTIPLE TARGETS. Such a mechanism is often used to assign a different format to the same contents, for example to generate HTML from well-formatted text. Such a mechanism could not be implemented without the separation of content and layout.

When you use a word processor, you'll probably find the separation of content and layout to be a bit arduous if you follow it to the last detail. In fact, even desktop publishing experts have been spotted overriding a paragraph layout once in a while when they felt the definition of an extra paragraph type wasn't justified. This is acceptable as long as it is an exception, and as long as you are aware that you are trading layout flexibility for

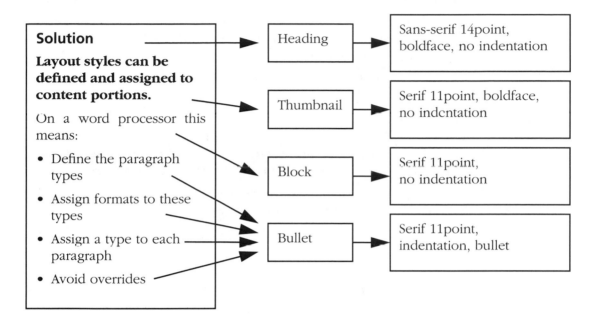

Figure 38. Separation of contents and layout as done by a word processor

momentary convenience. Ultimately, overrides break the concept of DOCU-MENT TEMPLATES and sacrifice its advantages. Whether a limited separation of contents and layout is justified or not depends on the likelihood and the frequency with which you are likely to have to react to requests for layout changes.

Single Source and Multiple Targets

Problem   **How can multiple views of a document be created without doubling maintenance?**

Forces   Sometimes the same document needs to appear in different formats. For example, we may require both a printable version and an HTML version of a document. Preparing a separate document for either format, however, leads to redundant documents.

Or consider comments in the source code describing, say, class interfaces on one side and an HTML API description on the other. Perhaps you cannot, or don't want to, sacrifice either. Again, redundancy occurs.

We can see from these scenarios that redundant information cannot always be avoided.

Redundancy, however, creates numerous problems – this is as true for documentation as it is for software. When information is stored redundantly in several places, document maintenance becomes expensive and error-prone. Changes have to be made several times and inconsistencies occur easily.

This is not what we aim for – clearly we don't want to maintain redundant documents and manually keep them consistent.

Fortunately there are ways to deal with redundancy. The key idea to understand is that all we need are multiple views of the same information, and that there is no need to keep more than one original.

Solution   **The documentation infrastructure can employ mechanisms that take source documents and automatically generate additional views. Such mechanisms avoid double maintenance and ensure consistency.**

While this technique does not avoid redundancy, it does manage it: only the source document has to be maintained.

The following mechanisms are prominent examples:

- Most word processors are capable of exporting HTML, as illustrated in Figure 39.

- Tools such as *JavaDoc* from the Java Developers Kit (Flanagan 2002) allow HTML to be generated from source code comments.

An interesting question remains: if you need several views of a document, which should be the source and which should be the targets?

A mechanism to generate a specific view can only lose structure on the way, so the view that offers the highest degree of structure must always be the source. For instance, a well-structured document is inherently more profoundly structured than an HTML document, so it is wise to use the document as the source and HTML as the target format. As a consequence, if you

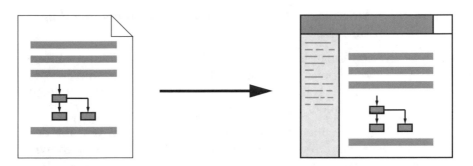

Figure 39. An HTML document generated from a text document

know you need both text and HTML, always maintain the text and generate the HTML.

Similarly, as source code comments are associated with code lines, and therefore feature a higher degree of structure than HTML, source code comments are extracted from the code and into HTML, and not vice-versa.

Discussion   Automatic document generation does not change a document's structure, just the document's format or its layout: the contents remain untouched. The precondition for this to work is that content and layout are not mixed in a document, but are properly separated. Therefore the feasibility of automatic document generation depends on the SEPARATION OF CONTENTS AND LAYOUT principle being adopted for the source document.

Mechanisms for document generation often have to assume that the sources are available at a certain place in the DOCUMENT ARCHIVE. A stable archive structure is therefore the precondition for this pattern to be useful. This can be achieved by permitting REORGANISATION UPON REQUEST only.

Import by Reference

Problem   **How can different documents use the same diagram or table consistently?**

Forces   Information contained in diagrams, pictures and tables is sometimes useful in the context of multiple documents. For example, a diagram describing the software architecture can turn out useful in an architecture overview, a design document and a usage concept.

If we include such information items in several documents, these items appear redundantly, bringing with it the well-known problems of redundancy: double maintenance, possible inconsistencies and so on.

However, generating documents in which these items appear is not a solution, as it is not the entire documents that are redundant, only small artefacts inside them.

Still, there is no need to store such pieces of information redundantly. All we need are multiple representations of the same information.

Solution   **Artefacts that need to appear in multiple contexts can be imported by reference into the documents that include them.**

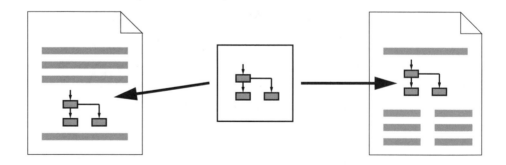

Figure 40. A graphic referenced by two documents

This technique is illustrated in Figure 40, and can be characterised as follows:

- The diagrams, pictures, tables and so on are stored in appropriate places.

- They are included in all documents wherever they are needed using the 'import by reference' mechanism that most word processors offer.

- If the original item is changed, all instances within those documents are updated automatically the next time the documents are opened.

Discussion   This technique avoids the maintenance problems associated with redundancy. However, it cannot be denied that there are several drawbacks associated with import by reference, which you have to weigh against its advantages when you consider using it.

First, if you refer to the artefact with text, that text will not be updated automatically when the artefact changes, which carries the danger of conflicting information in the diagram or table on one hand and the surrounding text on the other.

Next, if specific artefacts are needed in several documents, these documents overlap, at least to a certain degree. This can be an indication that such documents aren't properly focused, although not necessarily. If this *is* the case, you can try to avoid the situation altogether by striving for more FOCUSED INFORMATION, resulting in smaller overlaps.

Another disadvantage is that a document that references external artefacts requires several files, so that opening such a document might take more time than it otherwise would. Furthermore, using many referenced artefacts within a document is often a rather fragile construction, as the DOCUMENT ARCHIVE in which the items are stored might undergo a reorganisation. It helps here to implement REORGANISATION UPON REQUEST only, that is, to only reorganise the archive when it is actively requested by its users. Still, maintenance of documents with references to information items can be awkward.

To solve the last problem, you may consider importing artefacts by reference only as long as its main advantage applies: use import by reference while the artefacts are likely to change frequently, and replace the references by imported copies when changes become less likely and separate maintenance no longer appears a burden.

Separation of Processing and Printing

Problem   **How can projects produce useful, printable documents?**

Forces   Team members must be able to read and print each other's documents, whether they use the same tools or not, and independently of the platform on which the documents were produced. Moreover, customers and members of other teams who have access to the project documentation must also be able to read and print it.

However, other people sometimes aren't supposed to *modify* the documentation, so there should be a way to provide a document version that does not allow further processing.

Further, a document should look the same wherever it is printed. When a document is delivered, readers should not be able to override the layout and formatting, nor should the layout and formatting be overridden incidentally by, for example, the printer configuration.

Unfortunately, some word processors change documents automatically the moment they are opened. Worse, macros, font installations and printer configurations allow documents to look different on different systems. Under these circumstances the use of even simple formatting elements such as page breaks becomes a matter of pure chance.

In addition, opening a document can be unsafe when the document contains macros that are executed automatically, as macros can host viruses. Preferably, no macros should be executed when reading or printing a document.

Solution   **If a team chooses to deliver the project documentation in a print format that is widely available, all readers are able to print the documents, independent of the platform they use.**

The key to this solution is the clear separation of formats for document processing on one hand and print formats on the other. Teams should take care to distribute only versions of their documents in the print format whenever the recipients aren't expected to process the documents further.

In detail, print formats should meet the following requirements:

- Print formats must fully capture all information about the layout and formatting of a document. This includes the use of typefaces, the page geometry and so on. The page layout of the printed document must be part of the document alone, and must not depend on the surrounding infrastructure.

- Print formats must not allow further processing.

- Ideally, print formats should not allow macro execution either.

- To ensure the documentation is widely available, access to print formats must be free.

Discussion   The page description language PDF (Portable Document Format) is the most prominent example of a print format that completely and unambiguously describes the printed page. PDF is an excellent choice, as it can be read with the Adobe Acrobat Reader, a tool that is freely available for multiple platforms.

PostScript is another useful print format, as it can be read with GhostView – another free tool. However, PostScript is less widely used, and not as platform-independent as PDF.

Obviously, the use of a print format has an influence on the choice of a documentation tool. If you're responsible for setting up the documentation infrastructure, you might want to give preference to tools that *directly* support print formats, for example tools that generate PDF. Keep in mind, though, that FEW TOOLS should be sufficient for documentation purposes.

Document Templates

Problem   **How can all project documents acquire a reasonable structure and a good layout at little cost?**

Forces   We have seen that layout and formatting matter. A good layout makes a document more legible. Project documents must meet a certain degree of formatting standards.

However, it is inefficient to let the team members take care of things such as layout and formatting individually. Everybody would come up with their individual solutions, so there wouldn't be a consistent look and feel throughout the project documents. More importantly, it would be a waste of resources.

In an agile project, assuming an agile attitude, not everybody has the time to design document layouts. And even if several people took the time, they would end up doing similar things independently of each other.

Finally, it's likely that not everybody in the team has the knowledge to come up with a useful layout.

Reusing well-designed document layouts sounds like a good idea. However, it's not just the document layout that we can reuse.

Most projects have some experience with the typical contents of specific documents. They know what kind of materials should go into a requirement specification, or into a design document, and so on. It is worthwhile reusing this experience, so that team members need not re-invent the typical elements of a document they intend to write.

Solution   **Document templates, once they have been properly designed, impose their structure and layout on all documents that are produced using them.**

Almost all word processors allow templates to be used as the basis for new documents:

- A template defines the layout for all documents of a specific kind. The entire set of document templates defines a layout to be inherited by the project documents, as shown in Figure 41. Furthermore, the templates can ensure, at least to some general degree, a consistent look and feel over the entire project documentation.

- A template specifies the structure of all documents of a specific kind, or at least part of it. For example, a template may include the sections and subsections that all specification documents require, while leaving further structuring to the authors of the individual specifications. It can even include some sample text as a kind of prototype.

Ideally, one person, or a small group of people, can provide all necessary templates, and the rest of the team need not be concerned with any layout and formatting. Templates may even be available organisation-wide, so that a project can simply reuse the work of previous projects.

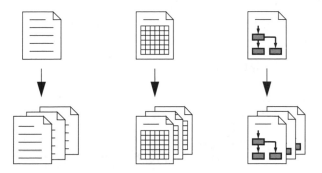

Figure 41. Document templates

Discussion   To make sure that templates lead to documents that are highly legible and aesthetically pleasing, the templates must follow the typographical patterns from Chapter 3, otherwise typographical mistakes and awkward layouts would be copied into many documents.

Next, templates must be easy to use. Often relatively simple templates do perfectly well. To a certain degree, their simplicity can be measured by how a template employs the SEPARATION OF CONTENTS AND LAYOUT: the template typically defines paragraph formats for the authors of the project documents to use. A small set of paragraph formats, say ten or so, is almost always sufficient. An extensive set of formats, however, makes templates complex and difficult to use.

How exactly can templates provide a tentative structure for a document? A template can introduce placeholders for the structural elements described in Chapter 2, in particular for GUIDELINES FOR READERS, for a GLOSSARY and for a DOCUMENT HISTORY.

Templates can do more than this, however. If you choose to have a template for each document from the DOCUMENTATION PORTFOLIO, you can set up sections for all topics that are normally dealt with in these documents.

Finally, for a collection of document templates to be generally available, they are best stored in a well-defined place inside the project's DOCUMENT ARCHIVE. To make sure that users find the templates easily, these archives should undergo REORGANISATION UPON REQUEST only.

Few Tools

Problem

How can projects minimise the effort spent on the introduction and use of documentation tools?

Forces

We want to produce high-quality documentation. Appropriate tools are necessary for producing, maintaining, printing, storing and retrieving documents. But which tools should we choose?

To this end, we have to remind ourselves that the introduction of tools brings with it a learning effort. Teams must familiarise themselves with tools before they can use them efficiently. The effort that goes into this can become quite large when a large number of tools is involved and, most importantly, when tools are complex in use. Complex tools can easily turn out to burden rather than support the users.

To make the last statement sound more positive: we can reduce the effort if we manage with fewer and simpler tools.

The effort associated with tools also depends on which tools the team members have used previously. Things are much easier if a team can rely on tools that many of the team members have been using for years.

Moreover, there is a cost advantage in using tools that are readily available within the organisation, as no licences for additional tools are necessary. This suits us well, as we don't want to spend an undue amount of money on the documentation infrastructure.

The cost argument, however, should not lead us to decide on tools that ultimately do not fulfil their purpose. The best cost advantage isn't worth much when the tool cannot provide the service that is needed.

Solution   **Almost all projects can manage with a small set of documentation tools.**
The following table gives a list of tools that a project may need.

Tool	Purpose
Word processor	Produce all texts that go into paper documents, including diagrams and tables
HTML editor	Produce Web pages, unless they can be generated
Digital camera	Capture the output of workshops and whiteboard discussions
Spreadsheet	Work on planning sheets
PDF reader	Read and print printer-ready documents
Web browser	Read on-line documents
Web site	Make the project documentation available
Configuration management	Store documents and document versions

When you have a choice of different products for each category, the following criteria can help you make a decision:

- Quality: tools must be reliable and easy to use.

- Availability: tools that are readily available in the organisation cost less than tools that need to be purchased.

- Cost: if quality and availability aren't the decisive factor, pay as little as you can.

The general guideline to follow is that tool support for documentation should be as simple as possible.

Sometimes projects are inclined to use more complex tools, such as CASE tools that also support documentation. Before a project makes a decision on such a tool, however, it must be able to explain why the tool is necessary, and how it helps the team more than simpler tools could.

Discussion   The Agile Manifesto gives preference to humans and interaction over processes and tools (as cited in Alistair Cockburn's book (Cockburn 2001)). This does not mean that there isn't any value in tools, but it reminds us that tools should serve people, not vice versa.

Scott Ambler recommends the use of the *simplest tools possible*, but comments that this is not always the same as *simple tools*. The appropriate degree of simplicity depends on the project's INDIVIDUAL DOCUMENTATION REQUIREMENTS.

One example of a simple tool is the digital camera mentioned in the table on page 143. It may surprise you to see it in the list of documentation tools, but it makes a lot of sense. A digital camera is easy to use, and can turn the results of whiteboard discussions into JUDICIOUS DIAGRAMS. This technique has been suggested in the literature on agile development (Cockburn 2001, Ambler 2002).

As far as word processors are concerned, make sure the tool you use supports PDF generation, preferably in a straightforward way. This is the easiest way to achieve a SEPARATION OF PROCESSING AND PRINTING. Also give preference to tools that take a technically sound approach to the SEPARATION OF CONTENTS AND LAYOUT, for example by offering a straightforward way to define paragraph formats.

Annotated Changes

Problem   **How can authors avoid confusion over changes they have made?**

Forces   While a document is still under development, changes are made frequently. This does not represent a problem, as long as only one person is involved in writing the document.

Documentation, however, can be a collaborative effort. Several people can contribute to a document as co-authors. Co-authoring a document is much more effective if all authors are aware of the recent changes the others have made.

Logging recent changes springs to mind as a solution, and most word processors offer such a feature. But as more changes are made, the size of the change logs grows and grows, and after a while the logs become too long to be useful.

Solution   **While a document is under development, authors can use automatic annotations to identify those parts of the document that have changed recently.**

Word processors offer the following techniques to track changes made to a document:

- Change bars on the outer margin indicate the paragraphs that have recently changed.

- New text can appear in different colours, even indicating the person who added the text.

- Text that has been deleted may still be visible, but crossed out.

- Annotations can be attached to text that say who last changed it and when.

Once a document has reached a stable state, is distributed among the team, or is even delivered to the customer, such annotations must be removed. Not only would they clutter the document and destroy the overall layout, they would be meaningless to most readers.

Discussion   This pattern is of great use when a document is written by co-authors as a joint effort. However, another pattern recommends that each document have ONE RESPONSIBLE AUTHOR. Is this a contradiction? No, it's not: co-authoring a document is perfectly natural. The job of the responsible author is to ensure that the document is written as intended, and if there are co-authors, that contributions are integrated smoothly. Change bars and annotations are there to help the responsible author.

Notification upon Update

Problem   **How can readers be prevented from using outdated versions?**

Forces   Information can expire, in particular in a project that has not yet been completed. New documents are added, existing documents are updated.

Normally we want our colleagues to read the most recent versions of our documents, since the most recent versions represent the best of our knowledge. But how can people know that there is a new document, or a new version of an existing document?

You can't expect people to check the archive regularly for new versions. And there is little benefit in asking people to use your documents on-line so that they get new versions automatically. Since print is the medium of choice for many documents, people will print those documents anyway, and changes would then go unnoticed.

So you have to inform people when a document has changed. But how detailed should the information be? Information about updates must be detailed enough for people to decide whether a new version is relevant for them.

However, it's not a good idea to send an e-mail message including the new version itself. This would only ensure that the document was stored redundantly many times in the recipients' mailboxes.

Solution   **Whenever there is a significant change in a project document, all potential readers should be notified of the new version. The notification should roughly explain what has been changed, but should not include the updated material itself.**

Often electronic mail is the method of choice to notify readers. The notification should include the following information:

- Which documents have been added or updated, and the relevant version numbers.

- Why the new version became necessary, and which material is new.

- A pointer to where the new versions can be found.

Discussion   Notifications become necessary as a consequence of doing CONTINUING DOCUMENTATION, caused by the need to develop software and documentation concurrently. The version number and the list of changes given in the notification should be synchronised with the DOCUMENT HISTORY listed in the document itself.

Before sending out the notification of a new version to readers, the author must ensure that the new version has been checked into the DOCUMENT ARCHIVE. The pointer to where the new version can be found is then a pointer to the location in the archive where the version is stored.

When new documents are added, informing potential readers may not be enough – the DOCUMENT LANDSCAPE may need to be updated as well.

Reorganisation upon Request

Problem

How can the documentation infrastructure be maintained?

Forces

A stable infrastructure is a key factor for useful documentation. Users expect documents to be stored in specific places, expect tools to work in a particular way and so on. Frequent reorganisation confuses everybody.

However, at some point reorganisation of the infrastructure can become inevitable. When a project starts the documentation infrastructure cannot be complete. As the project evolves, additional requirements for the infrastructure develop. Maybe the hierarchy in which the documents are organised needs to be extended, maybe additional document templates become necessary and so on.

However, reorganisation represents a fair amount of effort. Adapting access paths, checking if tools still work and so on are typical tasks that follow reorganisation. This makes reorganisation quite expensive.

Also, an infrastructure is hardly ever perfect; it can almost always be improved. This fact alone doesn't justify reorganisation. Making a useful infrastructure even better hardly ever pays off.

Experience shows that, when documentation management runs smoothly, users simply use the documentation infrastructure. When the documentation infrastructure is problematic to the point that reorganisation becomes inevitable, users actively ask for changes.

Solution

Frequent reorganisation makes things worse, not better. Reorganisation of the documentation infrastructure should take place only when it is actively requested by the members of the project team.

Reorganisation should meet the following preconditions:

- The expected benefits must justify the effort that is caused by the consequences for existing documents, tools or methods.

- Project efforts rise and fall in natural cycles, sometimes of a year, sometimes half a year. This period is a threshold time span during which it should be probable that further reorganisation will not be necessary.

In other words, if you're in charge of managing the documentation, you should take users' complaints about the documentation infrastructure seriously, but you shouldn't overreact to small problems that, while they may exist, are hardly crucial.

Discussion   Reorganising the documentation infrastructure has a number of consequences. It can affect the DOCUMENT TEMPLATES in two different ways. First, their location in the DOCUMENT ARCHIVE can change, and second, the templates themselves can be reorganised. The latter, if done while a project is in progress, can put the consistent layout of existing and future documents at risk.

Reorganisation also influences the use of tools. First, this is true for a configuration management system used in the DOCUMENT ARCHIVE, which at least needs its access paths adjusted. But perhaps also the archive hierarchy is affected: in this case the reorganisation must preserve, or re-create, the archive's structural clarity and balance.

Second, reorganisation affects mechanisms that automatically generate documents following the SINGLE SOURCE AND MULTIPLE TARGETS principle, as well as mechanisms for IMPORT BY REFERENCE. Again, access paths need to be updated.

Programming and documentation – an analogy

There is an interesting analogy between several of the patterns in this chapter and several programming principles.

- Setting up a DOCUMENT LANDSCAPE and implementing it using a DOCUMENT ARCHIVE resembles the principles of data structures and their physical representation. The fact that these are two patterns has its roots in the idea that specification and implementation should be separated.

- The SEPARATION OF CONTENTS AND LAYOUT contributes to decoupling, which adds to a document's flexibility. This is similar to the flexibility gained by a software system through decoupling components following the 'separation of concerns' principle.

- The discussion of formats in the SEPARATION OF PROCESSING AND PRINTING parallels the discussion of data exchange formats known from software engineering.

- The use of DOCUMENT TEMPLATES promotes reuse through a mechanism similar to inheritance. Document templates provide structures that are reused many times.

- Having a SINGLE SOURCE AND MULTIPLE TARGETS as well as the IMPORT BY REFERENCE technique avoid (or at least manage) redundancy by adding a level of indirection. A certain loss of efficiency is accepted in order to make maintenance easier. You can find the same trade-off in software development.

- The principle of NOTIFICATION UPON UPDATE greatly resembles event-based software architectures.

- REORGANISATION UPON REQUEST discusses the trade-off between the advantage of an improved organisation and the costs of reorganisation – a discussion that can be found in many software projects.

These principles are as important in documentation as they are in software engineering. Often people will not notice their application, and will only miss them when they are not applied. These principles help you pursue a straightforward programming style on one hand and a lean organisation of your documentation on the other.

Experience Reports

Let's now look at the documentation infrastructure of some of our sample projects. We'll see the different techniques that the projects used to organise their documentation, and we'll also see the problems they faced.

Storing and retrieving documents

If you look back at Figure 35 on page 118, you can see what a poorly organised project infrastructure looks like. So how does a well-organised DOCUMENT LANDSCAPE look like? Figure 42 shows how Project Contentis organised its documentation.

Contentis was a fairly small project, so the team chose a very simple solution for organising their documents. The documents were stored in the file system, and versioning merely consisted of adding version numbers to the document names. Despite, or perhaps because of, its simplicity, this solution worked very well.

In a larger project, however, a more elaborate solution probably makes sense. Project Persistor also chose to use the file system as the basis for its DOCUMENT LANDSCAPE, but recognised that it was necessary to have an underlying DOCUMENT ARCHIVE. Project Persistor was a development project, and a configuration management system was already in use for versioning software modules. It was only logical to use this system for the project documentation

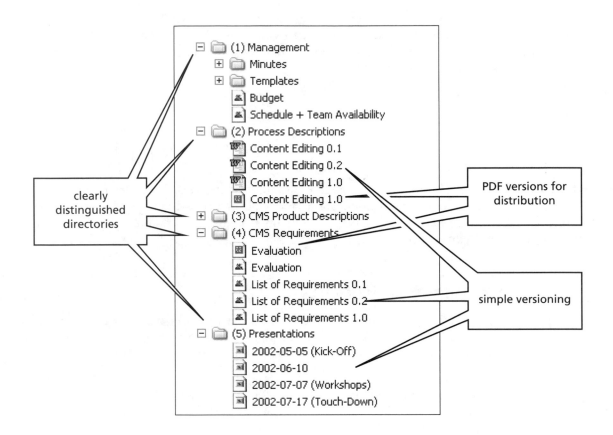

Figure 42. Project Contentis: a file system based document landscape

as well. Figure 43 shows the file system organisation, which mirrors the structure within the configuration management system, in which old versions aren't visible.

Project Navigator came up with yet another solution. This project used a CASE tool anyway, and stored several text documents within it. In addition, the project also felt a need for HTML documentation, to enable them to navigate through the descriptions of the component designs and the interface specifications. These HTML documents were placed in a project WIKI, as shown in Figure 44.

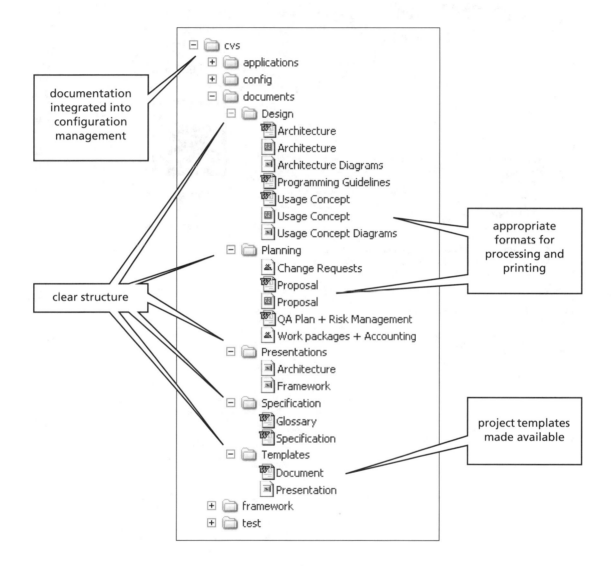

Figure 43. Project Persistor: Document landscape on top of configuration management

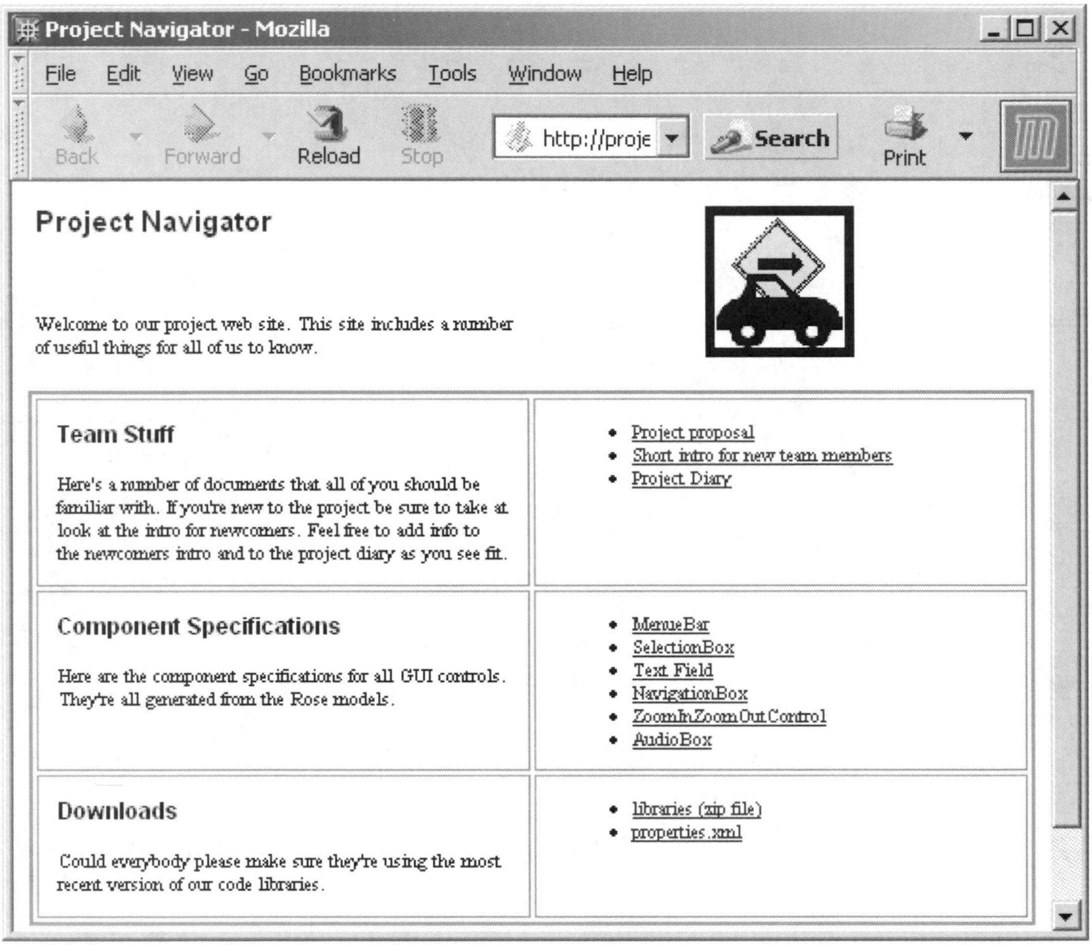

Figure 44. Project Navigator: a web-based document landscape

As different as these solutions are, they all have in common that they are well organised, clear and easy to memorise. You get a feel for the DOCUMENT LAND-SCAPE and you know where to look for each document.

All these examples also make use of READER-FRIENDLY MEDIA. Both Project Persistor and Project Contentis chose to produce documents intended for

Project Persistor: a simple file system structure

The infrastructure for all project files was set up as soon as the project had started. This included both project documents and source code. It was clear that the team would use a configuration management system for the code, so it was an easy decision to use the same system to archive the project documents as well.

The documents describing the data access layer framework were stored in well-organised file system directories that were accessible by the entire project team for reading and writing (Figure 43). The underlying configuration management system made sure that a document had to be checked out before anyone could change it, and that earlier versions could be retrieved if necessary.

print, and implemented this through PDF generation. As you can see in Figures 42 and 43, both projects provided PDF versions of the documents that were going to be distributed.

Project Navigator faced strong requests for navigation through the project documentation, and therefore supplied on-line versions of some documents. Project FlexiCar came to the same conclusion. This project decided to provide specific information on-line at the customer's request. In both cases, the high degree of referentiality had led to on-line documents as READER-FRIENDLY MEDIA.

Project FlexiCar: generating implementation documents

In addition to the design documents produced, the customer was interested in the documentation of the actual implementation.

JavaDoc was the perfect tool to generate this documentation without any additional effort. The team had supplied source code comments whenever necessary, and had followed the guidelines for Java comments from the start. An HTML commentary for all classes could therefore be generated at no extra effort.

Producing documents   This discussion takes us to the question of how these on-line documents were produced. The on-line documents, both in Project Navigator and in Project FlexiCar, included information that originated elsewhere. This was no problem, however, as in both cases the on-line versions could be generated automatically. Project Navigator generated its documents automatically from a CASE tool. Project FlexiCar had followed the principle of CODE-COMMENT

PROXIMITY and had supplied rich source code comments at the crucial points within the software, allowing JavaDoc to be employed.

This demonstrates the benefits that tools can bring very well: they can save extra work. Double work and double maintenance are things we clearly want to avoid – we don't want to document the same thing twice.

Project Vista gives another example how a tool can help in this case. Again, information had to be made available in different formats, and having a SINGLE SOURCE AND MULTIPLE TARGETS was the key to managing redundancy.

Project Vista: generating a table from a diagram

The diagram of the application landscape (Figure 7, page 54) revealed most of the dependencies between the systems the customer used. The diagram was maintained using Microsoft Visio, and was updated whenever the team gained more insight into the customer's application landscape.

The diagram was perfect for handing out and for getting discussions started. The diagram wasn't appropriate, however, for a more detailed description of the dependencies the team had identified. What was needed was a list of all dependencies, to which more information could be added and which allowed the dependencies to be classified.

The team decided to keep a list of all system dependencies in a Microsoft Excel spreadsheet. This spreadsheet was far too large to be maintained manually. One person wrote a small script that extracted the information about arrows that connected boxes in the Visio diagram and transformed this information into a format that could be imported into the spreadsheet.

This was a relatively easy mechanism that was implemented within a few hours. It worked efficiently enough to allow the spreadsheet to be updated on an almost daily basis.

However, Project Navigator also has a warning for us. It took this project a while before the documentation infrastructure was up and running, which caused some trouble. Once it was running, it was re-organised several times. People had to adjust tool configurations more than once. Instead of performing a REORGANISATION UPON REQUEST, unnecessary reorganisations used up resources that could have been spent better elsewhere.

Project Navigator: integrating design and documentation

The team really had mixed feelings about the documentation in this project.

The good part was that the project followed the strategy of documenting everything at most once. The customer had suggested the use of generation mechanisms to avoid the maintenance of redundant documents.

- Rational Rose was used as a modelling tool. For each component, the Rose model included a description, a class diagram and the interface specification. A code frame for each component could be generated automatically, which included source code comments for the interface methods.

- In addition, the customer wanted a small design document for each component. This document also consisted of the description, the class diagram and the interface specification, and was generated from the Rose model.

- Several developers felt that on-line versions of the design documents were helpful, as they used these components in their everyday programming. HTML pages were generated automatically and integrated into the overall web documentation the project had set up (Figure 44).

The drawback was that it took quite a while before the infrastructure was established.

First of all, it took time for a file system directory to be defined to which everybody in the team had access. This was mainly because the team worked on different sites. Until the problem was solved, team members resorted to circulating documents via e-mail whenever an update became available. People soon had lots of different versions of project documents in their mailboxes, which led to several conflicts in which someone used an outdated version.

Second, it took a while before all the generation mechanisms were up and running. Until this was done, the components' Rose model and design documents were maintained redundantly, despite an attempt to avoid this.

Finally, the infrastructure, and in particular the generation mechanisms, underwent frequent reorganisation. The team had to use different mechanisms several times, which caused a significant overhead.

Similarly, Project Paracelsus got into trouble because it took too long to make the documentation infrastructure available. In this case, the DOCUMENT TEMPLATES were missing. Project Persistor shows how this specific problem should be solved: the project templates are stored in the DOCUMENT LANDSCAPE along with all other materials (Figure 43).

Project Paracelsus: missing templates

When the team started writing the specification and the design documents, no templates for these documents were available because the organisation didn't provide any. The team had the choice of either designing a template on their own or doing without one.

A few weeks into the project, one person took the time to set up a simple document template. By this time, however, everybody had already been working on their documents, which had a rather inconsistent structure and layout as a result. Most of the documents lacked some of the elements that are useful to readers: guidelines, a document history and so on.

The documents were manually adapted to the new template. It was a small project with only a few documents, so the damage could quickly be repaired. Nevertheless, more time than necessary was spent in giving those documents an appropriate structure, let alone formatting and layout. Had the template been available from the start, the double work could have been avoided.

The conclusion we can draw from these examples is that a clear and effective infrastructure is the best technical support for documentation that you can have. The sooner the infrastructure is available, the better. DOCUMENT TEMPLATES are an essential part of this infrastructure, as are simple tools, providing that they avoid duplicated work.

Almost all projects can manage with FEW TOOLS, provided that the tools work reliably and efficiently. Of all the projects mentioned here, none relied on complex tools that were difficult to use. Simplicity and straightforwardness were strategies that worked well, while problems were caused by complexity, frequent reorganisation and infrastructures being implemented too late into the project.

I'd like to conclude this experience report with an example of how easy and how effective tool support can be. Among others, Alistair Cockburn and Scott Ambler recommend the use of a digital camera for documenting design discussions (Cockburn 2001, Ambler 2002): here is an example from Project

OpenDoors. It's the result of a whiteboard discussion that describes deployment processes for an Internet portal. It's a useful diagram, and it took only about ten minutes to commit it to paper.

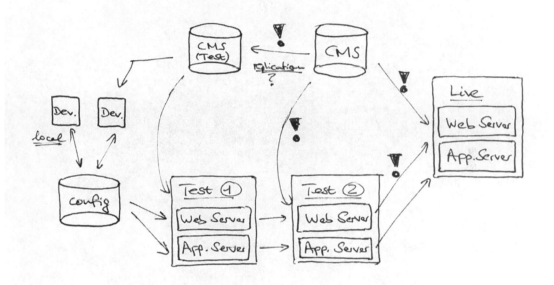

Figure 45. Project OpenDoors: a digital camera snapshot

5 Management and Quality Assurance

The value of documentation is only to be realized if the documentation is well done. If it is poorly done, it will be worse than no documentation at all.

Gerald M. Weinberg (Weinberg 1998)

Martin and Daniel, programmers, and Laura, the project manager, sat around in the cafeteria, drinking espresso and discussing the latest football results. Laura said: 'Oh yes, one thing I forgot about at the project meeting – what are we going to do about the documentation?' 'Hmm... you mean, we are supposed to do documentation?' 'Well, sure we are.' 'Ok, but can't we do that when we've completed the next code release? We've got absolutely no time for that now.'

The conclusion to draw from this story is not that you shouldn't plan the documentation for your project in the cafeteria. If you choose to sit down together in a nice atmosphere and plan your project with a cup of coffee in your hand, there's nothing wrong with that.

Neither is the conclusion that you should sacrifice the testing before code release, spend the time on documentation instead, and deliver software that hasn't been tested.

Still, something's wrong here. Documentation, when it gets that type of attention, probably doesn't even vaguely meet its purposes. Important documents are likely to be missing, because the project manager and the team forgot to plan the documentation in the first place. They're discussing documentation between other meetings and don't really take it seriously. This isn't a strategy that will ensure that documentation efforts are well-targeted. The documents

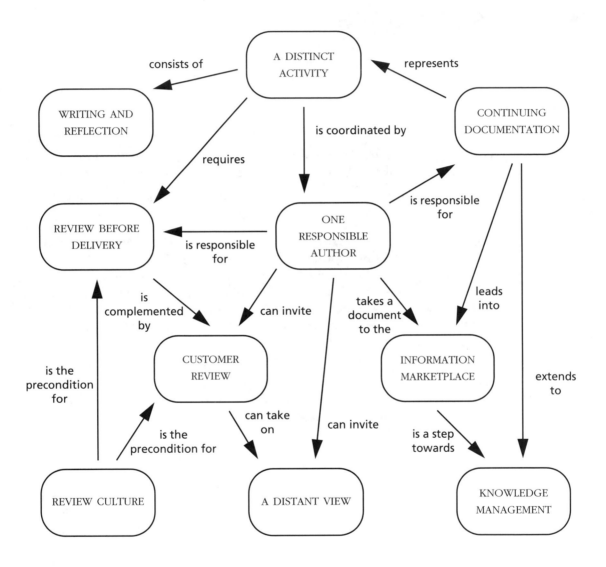

Figure 46. Patterns for management and quality assurance

that do get written might well end up as a bunch of 'write-once-read-never' documents, and so not offer any benefit to readers.

Documentation doesn't happen automatically. You have to see to it that documentation takes place, and that it takes place in a way that fits the needs of your project. Planning need not, and should not, be confused with a heavyweight methodology or even with a documentation bureaucracy. Planning simply means that you make the necessary decisions.

When you decide about the documentation you need to balance the following forces. On one hand, high-quality documentation requires time and effort, but on the other, time and effort are valuable resources that must be spent with care. The key is to make sure that the effort spent on document-ation is spent well.

One step is to identify the materials that really should go into written docu-ments. This has been much discussed in Chapter 1. The next step is to identify the people who should work on the documentation. Management should always be concerned with people, and documentation management is no exception. The team members' personal preferences and skills play a role here. How can the authors of the project documentation be supported? Yet another step is to involve quality assurance. These are issues the patterns in this chapter address.

It's time to state again that this book does not present a documentation method ready to be used by the project manager. The following patterns don't say who should write specific documents and at what time. Rather, they guide you to set up your own way of documenting projects and assembling expertise in your organisation. Figure 46 gives an overview.

A Distinct Activity

Problem   **How should resources be assigned to documentation activities?**

Forces   Documentation can be important for later project stages or for the next project. If we produce inaccurate documentation or ignore the document-ation requirements altogether, much of the expertise held by the team members will be lost. The result is that we'll need to re-invent things later, due to a lack of documentation in the first place.

However, documentation binds resources. These resources cannot be used for other things such as programming or testing. It is pointless to argue that documentation should be given as much time as possible. First, document-ation doesn't automatically get better when you spend more time on it. Second, documentation need not always be perfect.

Agile development suggests that documentation be sufficient, but no more than that. It's unacceptable if a development project ends up with a number of nice documents but without operational software when the deadline is due.

We should therefore spend a *reasonable* amount of time on the document-ation of our software projects. Spending time on documentation must be justified by the expected benefits.

But what is a reasonable amount of time? There is no general answer to this question, since projects differ a lot – a development project is likely to have different demands on documentation than a consultancy project, for example.

A well-known psychological phenomenon makes the matter even more diffi-cult. Many people are reluctant to invest in something that only pays off later. This phenomenon is even more marked if only others will profit. If you spend time writing project documents, it's not necessarily you who will profit from those documents – more likely your colleagues or your customers will. Moreover, even if you profit from the documents yourself, you have to invest time now, but won't get any benefit until later.

All this calls for planning, and the planning must take into account the bene-fits that documentation has for the entire project, both now and in the future. This may seem obvious, but too many projects have ended up with poor documentation because they didn't plan documentation properly in the first place.

Planning, however, isn't restricted to assigning a budget. A budget isn't worth much when a team is too busy with other project activities – which always have higher priority. Documentation needs a *reasonable* budget and a *reasonable* priority, whatever 'reasonable' means in a specific project.

Solution

When documentation is considered a distinct project activity, and not just the by-product of coding, it can be assigned its own budget, priority and schedule. Documentation can then be weighed against other project activities.

The core idea is to make the assignment of resources to documentation *explicit*, and open to discussion, individually for each project. Exactly what budget is reasonable differs greatly, depending on the type of project. The important thing is to understand that documentation is one activity among others, and that similar to other activities, one that uses up resources.

- The project manager normally keeps a list of all project activities with a budget assigned to each activity, adding up to the total project budget. All documentation activities should be on that list, and a budget (time and resources) should be assigned to each.

- Moderated by the project manager, the team should assign priorities to all activities due in the near future. Documentation activities, if taken seriously, will be given a high priority at some points and a lower priority at others. The project manager should see to it that, over the course of the project, documentation receives the priority it needs when compared to other project activities.

- The team should also agree on a schedule for the documentation, and fix a delivery date for the next version of each document needed.

Customers often expect documentation to be delivered at various points throughout a project. Of course, you need to take this into account when you plan documentation activities.

Discussion

The time and budget you'll need for documentation clearly depends on the amount of documentation that's necessary. Because projects have INDIVIDUAL DOCUMENTATION REQUIREMENTS, the effort you have to spend can vary greatly. Choosing the necessary documents from the DOCUMENTATION PORTFOLIO, combined with a healthy dose of scepticism when it comes to large amounts of paperwork, will allow you to determine the resources you'll need, and to keep them within reasonable limits.

Determining the necessary amount of documentation actively and explicitly is a strategy also recommended in the literature on agile development. Alistair Cockburn does not make any assumptions about what or how much documentation a project needs, but he requires a team to pose and answer this question, for example through a planning game (Cockburn 2001).

There are more aspects to managing documentation than budget and priority. Another issue is to provide an environment that allows authors to treat documentation as a mix of WRITING AND REFLECTION. Moreover, a REVIEW CULTURE needs to be established that enforces the REVIEW BEFORE DELIVERY rule. Last but not least, it is essential to appoint ONE RESPONSIBLE AUTHOR for each document – preferably someone who enjoys doing documentation.

One Responsible Author

Problem   **How many people should be responsible for a document?**

Forces   If a large number of people are responsible for one task, it is likely that the task will not be done at all – everybody will think that someone else is in charge.

Responsibilities are clearer if only one person, or at most a small team, is responsible for any task. One idea is to have someone work on the project documentation full-time, since this person could then focus on the job.

Perhaps the project, however, can't spare one person for long enough to write the documentation alone, or no one person has enough knowledge to do so. Moreover, someone who exclusively works on documentation isn't involved in any other project activities. It's easier to produce good documentation when you are actively involved in a project rather than just observe it. This suggests that several people may have to contribute to the documentation.

As people are different, they have different interests and skills. Some software engineers dislike writing documentation and prefer the more technical tasks, while others quite like it. If we are interested in high-quality documentation, we must make sure that authors are skilled and motivated. What's the point in forcing someone to do the job who isn't inclined to do it?

Solution

For each project document, there must be one person who accepts responsibility for it. This person need not write the document alone, but must coordinate the contributions from other people.

The responsible person should be a member of the project team, have good writing skills and also enjoy writing (Weir 1997). That person should do the following:

- Collect material and arrange brainstorming sessions with other team members.

- Set up the overall document structure.

- Commit material to paper.

- If there are co-authors (which will sometimes be the case), solicit contributions from the co-authors and integrate these contributions, while ensuring a consistent writing style for language, diction and lines of argument.

- Arrange for document reviews and incorporate feedback from the reviewers.

Different project documents typically have different responsible authors, to ensure that for each responsible author the workload of documentation doesn't get too great in proportion to other project activities.

Discussion

This pattern is a special rendition of a general management principle. Among his patterns of project management risk reduction, Alistair Cockburn stresses that in a project there must be exactly one *Owner Per Deliverable* (Cockburn 1998), otherwise several people might work on the same thing, or important tasks might be neglected. This principle applies to documents as much as to all other types of deliverables, hence the requirement that the responsibility for a document be devolved to one person.

This responsibility includes establishing a process to ensure CONTINUING DOCUMENTATION, and arranging for a REVIEW BEFORE DELIVERY.

Continuing Documentation

Problem   **When should project documentation be written?**

Forces   It is clear that at the beginning of a project we are unable to document every-thing that we would like to see documented by the end. We don't yet know what the software architecture will look like, let alone more detailed design aspects. Of the things that we could describe already, such as user require-ments, at least some are likely to change as the project evolves.

However, we cannot postpone documentation until the project is finished. Documentation is needed for communication with customers and between team members. It has to be available during the project.

These points suggest that documentation should be started early in the project, at a relatively coarse-grained level, and should be continued, refined and updated regularly. For example, a design document can begin as a mere sketch and can be extended as the design evolves.

The question, however, is what we mean by 'regular' updates. On one hand, if we wait too long before documents are updated, readers are likely to be irritated by outdated information. Inaccurate information can be the source of serious misunderstandings, and can therefore do a lot of harm.

Worse still, excessively long time spans between documentation updates create the danger of the updates never being carried out at all. At some point, updating the documentation is easily forgotten. This clearly isn't what we want, as it would render the documentation useless in the long term due to inaccuracy.

All this suggests that we should be fairly quick with updates. If we wait until problems arise with outdated documents, we have waited too long – the damage has been done.

On the other hand, if documentation is updated immediately whenever a project detail changes, it will have to be modified almost continuously. This is expensive – documentation will require much more attention than necessary.

Moreover, updating documentation too frequently ensures that most of the time no stable documentation is available. This is in conflict with our desire to have *useful* documentation, however incomplete, from the beginning of the project.

Solution   **Project documentation, when it evolves continuously as the project goes on, offers the advantage that it reflects the last stable state of the project.**

Continuing documentation calls for documentation to be updated at regular intervals. What time frame you can assume for these regular intervals depends on the individual project:

- It is often a good idea to update the documentation with new software releases, thereby keeping the time scale of software and documentation releases in sync.

- The frequency of updates also depends on the type of document. More general documents, such as architecture descriptions, are more stable and need fewer updates than, for example, an interface specification, which may change daily in a busy project.

- Updates can be less or more urgent. An important document, one that is used on a day-to-day basis, must be updated quickly when its object has changed. A different document may be used less frequently: updating this document is not so urgent and can perhaps wait.

The existing documentation, in its perhaps intermediate state, should be made available to all team members, to allow them to use it as the project progresses.

Discussion   The Agile Manifesto recommends release cycles for software from a couple of weeks to a couple of months (in one of its concrete recommendations, as cited in Alistair Cockburn's book (Cockburn 2001)). Preference is given to a shorter timescale so that software delivery isn't slowed. A couple of weeks also sounds like a good *average* time frame for updating documents, although shorter as well as longer intervals can make sense.

Between updates, the documentation is not entirely up to date. Is this a problem, and is there something we can do about it? The first thing to do is to keep a DOCUMENT HISTORY, so that readers are aware of potential inaccuracies. Otherwise, people can overcome this problem by using a simple technique that Charles Weir suggests among his *Patterns for Designing in Teams*: all team members can keep a printed copy of the documentation and make *Ad-hoc Corrections* (Weir 1997) until the next version is distributed to the team.

Fortunately, many of the documents that undergo rapid change are those that people use to look up information – documents that are typically presented on-line (see READER-FRIENDLY MEDIA). These documents can often be generated. On the other hand, paper documents often put a FOCUS ON LONG-TERM RELEVANCE, which clearly reduces the problem.

To make continuing documentation possible, documentation must be considered A DISTINCT ACTIVITY – an integral part of a project that requires personnel capacity and a budget, just like all other project activities. For each document, the team must decide on the update frequency, and the ONE RESPONSIBLE AUTHOR should ensure that the update frequency is met.

Because the documentation is written and used while the project progresses, it is open to the REVIEW CULTURE that the project hopefully has established. This is a two-fold issue. First, writing documentation can provide insight into the software, as WRITING AND REFLECTION can go hand in hand. For example, when you describe a design, you implicitly validate it, much as you do when you explain it to others. This way, the documentation can contribute to the quality of the software. Second, as the documentation is used during the project, team members can give feedback concerning the quality of the documentation itself.

Writing and Reflection

Problem
How can documentation and other project activities stimulate each other?

Forces
Good ideas take time. Documentation is a creative process, and creative processes need time to allow ideas to develop and mature. A pre-requisite for a well-written text is that the author is given time for reflection during the writing.

This is even truer for documentation in conditions of rapid change. Evolving projects normally go hand in hand with piecemeal growth of the documentation, which requires authors to reflect on the changes and adaptations they need to make.

Authors do not only reflect upon the documents they write, they also reflect on the subject matter. Documentation is an important means of validation. You can gain insight for example into a software design while you document it, and notice things that are imperfect or incomplete. Writing documentation provides feedback on what is being documented.

In some cases, reflection can be the main purpose of a document. Some people get their best ideas in conceptual work when they try to commit the concept to paper. If someone works on a document with the purpose of thinking a concept or an idea through, it is crucial to take the time needed for new ideas and reflection.

Time isn't everything, however. Authors also require an environment that allows them to concentrate on their work. A member of the project team, the author typically deals with many other people, develops software, takes part in discussions, meetings and workshops and so on. That's fine, but when it comes to documentation, a little peace and quiet can do a lot of good. The importance of teamwork notwithstanding, a room with many people around isn't an environment that allows a person to concentrate on writing.

Solution

To get the best out of documentation, team members have to spend time on the actual writing, as well as in reflection on what they have written, preferably in an undisturbed environment.

This can be broken down into the following concrete advice:

- Collecting material and structuring that material involves creativity. It is almost impossible to write a perfect document straight off. The choice of material and the definition of an initial document structure have to be the subject of reflection. You have to expect the contents and the structure of a document to go through several steps of refinement before the document is completed.

- While writing, you should check the documentation for problems and inconsistencies. If you observe that parts of the documentation are problematic, this may suggest that it is the subject of the documentation that is itself problematic. In this way you obtain feedback on the project itself.

- Most people cannot reflect immediately upon what they have just written. – they need to gain a little distance. You should therefore let any writing process extend over a period long enough to allow ideas to develop in the back of your mind. This doesn't mean that you'll spend more time on documentation. Just plan to take a break, and to do other things in between, before you complete a document.

- For the purpose of documentation, team members should be given the opportunity to retreat to their own office, undisturbed by other team members or customers.

Figure 47 expands on the idea that documentation can become a means of validation. In a style similar to UML sequence diagrams, with time flowing from top to bottom, the diagram shows how the design and the document-ation processes evolve to produce their final results. Documentation, consisting of writing and reflection, is performed at regular intervals, and supplies feedback to the design process, which continues uninterrupted.

Discussion   In most projects it is appropriate to reserve regular time frames for document-ation and reflection. One idea is to spend four days a week designing, coding, having meetings and discussions, perhaps working at the customer's site, but to reserve one day per week for documentation and reflection in a quieter environment. Such a policy allows for CONTINUING DOCUMENTATION.

Since documentation is A DISTINCT ACTIVITY, its budget and priority can be high or low, depending on the project, so the 'four day vs. one day' rule might not always be appropriate. In many cases, however, it represents a fine balance between software development on the one hand and documentation and reflection on the other.

Finally, the need for a quiet environment doesn't mean that you should write documentation in isolation. Only an appropriate REVIEW CULTURE allows you to conduct a REVIEW BEFORE DELIVERY among the team, or a CUSTOMER REVIEW, which gives you the necessary input from others.

Review Culture

Problem   **How can the quality of the project documents be improved?**

Forces   Hardly anybody manages to write good documents without help from others. This is too much to ask – nobody is that smart. Documents need reviews, just as software needs testing.

Unfortunately, many reviews only mention what's wrong with a document, while the good things go unnoticed. People are, to varying degrees, afraid of criticism, and authors sometimes feel reluctant to have their documents reviewed. They might be afraid that their work is considered faulty when it is laid out before the critics' beady eyes, or they might be afraid of the extra

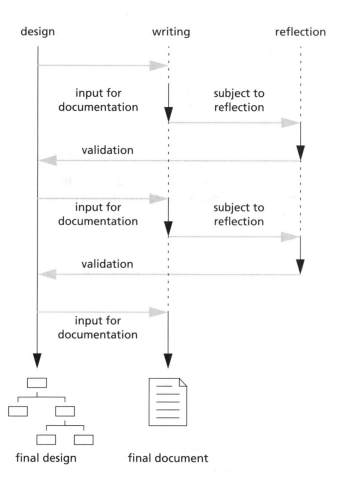

Figure 47. Documentation as a means of validation

effort of incorporating feedback into their work. Reviews can be tricky, so it's important to find ways to make reviews a positive experience both for the author and for the reviewers.

Most people accept criticism much better if it is clear that the criticism is intended to help them, not to put them down. To achieve this goal, a review must not be restricted to negative feedback, but must also have positive comments to make, and the review must offer concrete suggestions for improvement along with its critical remarks (Coplien 2000).

As well as this psychological issue, there is also a practical point that suggests that a review should include both positive and negative feedback. Authors are sometimes unsure about whether to keep or to replace specific material. Suggestions for either approach – keep or replace – can be helpful. But when a review doesn't mention what is good, the author might end up replacing material that really should have been left as it was. An all-negative review leaves the author in the dark and is not very helpful.

Solution
Documentation can profit a lot from reviews, provided a review culture has been established in which both authors and reviewers feel comfortable.

A positive review culture requires the following:

- Team members must be willing to discuss material and provide feedback when their expertise is required. They must understand their role as one of providing a service to the author.

- Reviewers must force themselves to be honest and must come up with clear comments about the quality of the material. They must mention both what they feel is good about the document and should be kept, and what they feel is not so good and which needs improvement.

- Along with critical comments, reviewers should make concrete suggestions for improvement whenever possible.

- Team members offering feedback must receive the acknowledgement and credit they deserve.

- Authors must be willing to accept feedback, knowing that the feedback will enable them to write a much better document.

- When another document is written, colleagues may choose to mutually change the roles of author and reviewer.

A positive team spirit, often underpinned by social events or casual out-of-office activities, helps team members to understand that they're all in the same boat. This isn't only true for documentation, it is true for all project tasks, and documentation is no exception.

Discussion   Review culture, and teamwork in general, has been the subject of much attention in the literature.

Several books that place emphasis on human issues in computing acknowledge the importance of teamwork in all aspects of software development. Gerald Weinberg, in his book on *The Psychology of Computer Programming*, speaks of 'ego-less' programming (Weinberg 1998). Frederick Brooks, in *The Mythical Man-Month*, (Brooks 1995), and Tom DeMarco and Timothy Lister in *Peopleware* (DeMarco Lister 1987), also provide plenty of insight into teamwork.

Teamwork, reviews, reflection and feedback also play an enormous role in the agile world. The Agile Manifesto, in one of its concrete recommendations, suggests that at regular intervals teams reflect on how they can become more effective, then tune and adjust their behaviour accordingly (Cockburn 2001). Several agile methods elaborate on this (Cockburn 2001, Ambler 2002, Schwaber Beedle 2001).

Norman Kerth, in his book *Project Retrospectives*, describes in detail what reflection meetings can be like, and gives many examples (Kerth 2001).

Neil Harrison's *Organisational Patterns for Teams* (Harrison 1996) stress the importance of team spirit to all team activities. A *Unity of Purpose* – sharing a common goal – is crucial for a team to work well together.

In his book *Writers' Workshops*, Richard Gabriel describes a review culture that is quite common among authors of prose and poetry, and one that has been adopted by the patterns community for reviewing software patterns (Gabriel 2002). A writers' workshop is an event specifically designed to allow authors to give each other intense feedback on their work.

Jim Coplien has described this review culture in his *Pattern Language for Writers' Workshops* (Coplien 2000). He claims that authors and reviewers must form a *Community of Trust* in which critical comments are useful, rather than just cause irritation. Jim Coplien asks that, for criticism to be practically useful, concrete *Suggestions For Improvement* be offered with each critical remark. He also emphasises the importance of having *Positive Feedback First*, since for psychological reasons, critical comments are more readily accepted after positive feedback has been provided.

None of these insights into teamwork apply exclusively to documentation. Most of the ideas apply to software development in general, whereas the ideas for writers' workshops are, within the software engineering context, mainly targeted towards the discussion of software patterns. However, what all the people mentioned above had in mind when they wrote about team-work was to empower teams to collaborate on a common goal. This is something from which documentation can also profit.

Review Before Delivery

Problem

How can authors receive the right feedback at the right time?

Forces

We know that documents need to be reviewed. However, we also know that reviews use up resources, and that unnecessary reviews should be avoided for economical reasons. To what extent are reviews necessary?

This depends on several factors. First, the author's familiarity with the subject, and the author's writing experience, both have an influence on how much a review is needed.

Next, the document's status plays an important role. Documents that describe work in progress cannot be expected to be complete, as they will undergo change. It is perfectly acceptable to circulate such documents amongst colleagues who understand that they are preliminary documents.

Official reviews for preliminary versions don't make sense. Nonetheless, feed-back on a preliminary version can help shape the scope and the overall structure of a document right from the start.

At some point, however, documents are officially distributed – perhaps just among the team, or perhaps to the customer, with a software release. Such documents must meet higher quality standards.

Solution

Early reviews are fine as they help the author shape the scope and the structure of a document. But before a document is officially distributed, or delivered to the customer, a review is mandatory.

Only the author can decide to what degree early or intermediate reviews are useful. In most cases an informal review is sufficient to give the author early feedback.

The final review is not up for debate. As a general rule of thumb, no document should be released to uninvolved readers until it has passed a final review.

This review should take place well before the document's planned distribution date, to allow time for revisions, and should address the following questions:

- Does the document meet its goals, and will it be of use to the readers?

- Is the document technically accurate, and does it provide the right level of technical detail?

- Is the overall structure and organisation right?

- Does the document provide enough examples to be comprehensible?

- What about layout and language?

Discussion   Reviews don't happen automatically. It is the responsibility of the document's ONE RESPONSIBLE AUTHOR to make sure that reviews take place and to ensure that the feedback is incorporated.

Obviously, the responsible author may disagree with what a reviewer says, or different reviewers may have conflicting opinions. Ultimately, the responsible author not only has to see to it that the feedback is incorporated, but is also free to decide *how* the feedback is incorporated.

The need for this pattern stems largely from the idea of CONTINUING DOCUMENTATION. In the early stages of a project it is too early to review the details of any documents. As the release date for the software draws nearer and a document is supposed to be completed, this is also the time to plan the final review.

Reviews are mainly concerned with the contents of a document. In addition, reviewers can check the quality of presentation. Especially, they can examine how well a document addresses the TARGET READERS, how well it presents FOCUSED INFORMATION, and the quality of REALISTIC EXAMPLES.

Customer Review

Problem   **How can a team use documentation to increase customer involvement?**

Forces   In any project it is the team, and not the customer, who is in charge. The team is expected to deliver results, and documentation is no exception.

Teams are therefore inclined to make progress fast, so that they have results they can deliver. Yet customer involvement is necessary. First, the project stakeholders are interested in how the project is progressing, and involving them is a way to keep them informed. Second, the customer is clearly knowledgeable, especially in the application domain, and can contribute much to make the project more successful.

Documentation is one area where customers can be involved. Handing out documentation to the stakeholders is one way to show them where the project is heading. On the other hand, the customer can also provide valuable feedback on the documentation.

This all can be summarised by saying that the better the collaboration with the customer, the better are the chances for a successful project.

Solution   **Customer reviews can improve the quality of a document, especially as far as the domain expertise is concerned, and at the same time add to team building and integration.**

The following guidelines help make customer review successful:

*   The customer must be made aware that the document under review is a draft. The document should clearly say so, because otherwise it can be mistaken for a final but badly done document.

*   A draft shouldn't be too tentative. As a team member, you cannot expect the customer to do your job and turn a collection of raw materials into a document for you.

A customer review can spawn important discussions, and can contribute much to making a project a joint effort in which the team and the customer work together towards a common goal.

Discussion   Customer collaboration is one of the core values of the Agile Manifesto. It has been much stressed in the literature on agile development, and more generally in the literature on effective project teamwork. For example, Jim Coplien, in his *Generative Development-Process Pattern Language* (Coplien 1995), recommends that projects *Engage Customers*, especially, though not exclusively, for purposes of quality assurance.

In her *Customer Interaction Patterns*, Linda Rising discusses this topic in detail (Rising 2000a). Among other things, she recommends that teams learn to *Know The Customer*, and that they *Listen, Listen, Listen* to what the customer says. Having the documented concepts reviewed by the customer clearly contributes to the desired customer collaboration.

For a customer review to work smoothly, the team and the customer have to establish a REVIEW CULTURE in which such reviews are considered normal, and in which no individual team member has reason to feel offended by criticism. The customer must acknowledge the team's need for feedback, and must not blame the team for not being experts in the application domain. The customer must understand that the request for a review is one way to ensure the quality of the project's results.

A Distant View

Problem   **How can authors obtain unbiased feedback?**

Forces   Reviewers who are all too familiar with a document under review are likely to have a somewhat biased view. They might take a lot of things for granted that might be questioned by an unbiased reviewer, and so may fail to come up with a reliable assessment.

This is often the case when team members act as reviewers. It is generally fine to have team members review project documentation, but sometimes they are so immersed in the project that they take the project's fundamentals for granted. What seems to be self-evident to the team can still be sophisticated to non-experts.

Moreover, project documents are often reviewed by people with a technical background. These reviewers tend to focus on the technical contents of a document but overlook presentation issues. However, the quality of presentation also deserves attention.

Solution   **Authors can obtain unbiased feedback from reviewers who are interested in the topic and who are generally knowledgeable in the field, but who are not involved in the actual work described in the document.**

Good candidates for a distant-view review are:

- Someone from outside the team who is familiar with the application domain.

- The customer, who can often take a slightly different perspective.

- To a lesser degree, a reviewer from inside the team with a different educational background.

Normally such people aren't going to focus on technical details in their reviews – and indeed, really shouldn't. Rather, it is their job to comment on the overall structure of a document, its general 'big picture' and on whether they feel the document generally addresses the right issues.

Discussion   Actually there are two kinds of reviews that complement each other. For the benefits of a REVIEW CULTURE to fully materialise, feedback at different levels is needed. On one hand, close colleagues who are familiar with the material presented can provide helpful comments on a more technical level. On the other, people from outside the team, perhaps the TARGET READERS, can take a distant view and provide valuable high-level comments. If it's the customer who takes the distant view, keep the guidelines for a CUSTOMER REVIEW in mind.

The recommendation to bring in someone from outside the team is commonly found in the literature. In his *Generative Development-Process Pattern Language* (Coplien 1995), Jim Coplien deals with the issue of design reviews. He suggests hiring a *Mercenary Analyst* from outside the team who is an expert in the domain and who can provide feedback. This is an important principle, not only for design reviews, but also for project documentation reviews.

In the *Creator-Reviewer* pattern from the *Patterns for Designing in Teams* (Weir 1997), Charles Weir explains that detailed knowledge of the application domain is an important requirement for a reviewer. He also recommends that reviewers not be involved in the work under review.

Finally, this pattern also corresponds to an observation described in Neil Harrison's *Organisational Patterns for Teams* (Harrison 1996). *Diversity of Membership* states that mixed teams – teams with people of different ages and gender, as well as with different educational and cultural backgrounds – generally perform better than more homogenous teams, since the team members complement each other. As far as the review process is concerned, the best feedback can be expected from reviewers with different backgrounds, both to each other and to the author.

Information Marketplace

Problem   **How can good documents be prevented from going sadly unnoticed?**

Forces   Producing documents alone is not enough. The best document in the world isn't worth much if it doesn't reach the intended readers. There is no point in completing a document, putting it in the archives and waiting for other team members to come across it. This would be the right strategy only if all you intended for a document was to use it as an excuse when the project goes astray, for example like arguing: 'This isn't my fault, I have documented it all.'

Such an attitude is the exact opposite to being agile. In an agile context, we don't want the project documents to serve as excuses, we want them to facilitate communication among the team. This means that we have to actively address team members and let them know that there is a document that might help them with their work.

Yes, there are technical options to make documents easily available, and there are technical ways to distribute documents among a team. It's fine to use these possibilities, and they are the first step to making documentation an effective means of communication. But you can take an important second step by addressing the intended readers directly.

Solution   **Documents gain more attention if the intended readers are actively invited to read them.**

There are different ways in which you can approach other team members when an important document has been finished and is being made available:

- You can mention the document at a team meeting, give a brief introduction to what the document says and invite the team to contact you whenever questions remain unanswered.

- You can pin a printed copy on the project notice board.

- You can send a brief e-mail message to the team in which you explain the purpose of the document and where it can be found.

In any case, documentation profits greatly from an atmosphere in which information is freely exchanged, and in which people let others know of any documents that might help them.

Discussion   This pattern seems similar to the idea of letting colleagues know of a new version through a NOTIFICATION UPON UPDATE. The emphasis of this pattern, however, is not on any kind of technical support, but rather on the attitude people take towards documentation. This pattern reminds us that, when we have completed a document, we are supposed to take the document to the TARGET READERS.

One of the implementation options for this pattern – pinning an important document to the project notice board – is closely related to what Alistair Cockburn calls an 'information radiator'. In *Agile Software Development*, he suggests that each project use an information radiator that displays information in a place where passers-by can see it (Cockburn 2001). If a team is used to electronic communication, you can also choose to put the document on the project WIKI and stick a message to it for all team members to see.

Adopting a culture of free information exchange in projects paves the way for an agile attitude towards dealing with information beyond the projects. If we regard documentation as something that is actively distributed, we meet the precondition for successful, organisation-wide KNOWLEDGE MANAGEMENT.

Knowledge Management

Problem   **How can future projects profit from a successful project?**

Forces   No two projects are the same. Nevertheless, projects do have things in common. There are analogies and similarities. We've all been in situations in which we had to find a solution to a problem, well aware that others must have solved a similar problem before. If only we could learn about their solution, we might save time and effort.

Almost all projects can profit from experience gained in previous projects. But we can draw on this experience only if it is made available within the organisation. Documentation is one way to do this, as it commits expertise to paper and saves it for future use.

However, even the best documentation isn't useful if no-one knows it exists, or no-one has access to it. All too often, new projects re-invent things, not because previous projects didn't document them, but because people aren't aware that the information is available.

Solution

Only when project documentation is made available organisation-wide do future projects have a chance of drawing on the expertise gained.

This has both a technical and a cultural aspect:

- Making the documentation available requires some kind of knowledge management system, as illustrated in Figure 48. Perhaps this is a publicly available directory, perhaps it's an intranet.

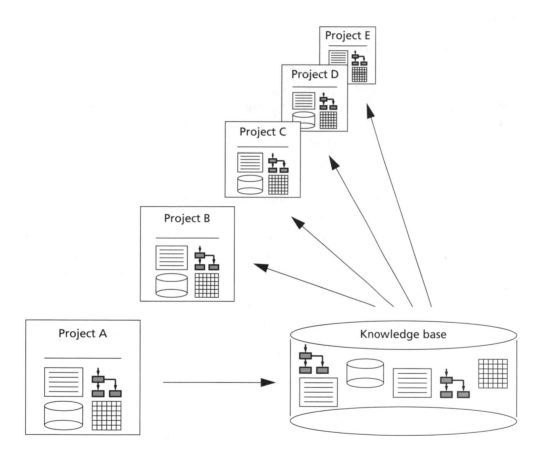

Figure 48. Extracting knowledge and passing it on

- The cultural aspect is more important. Using documentation for knowledge management can prove useful only in a culture that encourages people to share their experiences. Informal communication plays an enormous role here. As a project member, tell colleagues that the documentation exists. Invite people to examine it and to come back to you if they have questions. Make it clear there is a chance that others can profit from your work.

Discussion   Technically, what this pattern suggests is the integration of the project's DOCU-MENT LANDSCAPE into a landscape of documents that are relevant to the whole organisation. If you use an intranet this is particularly easy, turning your project WIKI into an in-house WIKI.

Here is where the documentation cycle closes. You have been busy doing CONTINUING DOCUMENTATION throughout your project, you have gone through stages of WRITING AND REFLECTION, and the REVIEW CULTURE has allowed you to profit from the knowledge of your colleagues.

Now the expertise that you have acquired can become useful for others. This is true in particular for material that places a FOCUS ON LONG-TERM RELEVANCE, such as documents conveying THE BIG PICTURE of the architecture, or the DESIGN RATIONALE.

At this point, you have produced a number of documents in your project. There shouldn't be too many of them. The previous patterns in this book will have guided you to a focus on the right topics, and to making the document-ation well-organised and lightweight. Now you and others can profit from work that was done. This is the idea of agile documentation.

Experience Reports

I'd like to conclude this chapter with by examining the documentation proc-esses in several example projects, and how these processes met or failed to meet the patterns in this chapter.

Processes   The Agile Manifesto favours individuals and interactions over processes and
and plans   tools, and responding to change over following a plan. Again, the manifesto does not deny the value of processes and plans. But it warns us not to follow a plan for the plan's sake.

Project Persistor gives a good example of what a lightweight documentation process can look like. The team was well aware that a certain degree of documentation was crucial to the project's success, regarded documentation as A DISTINCT ACTIVITY, and included the documentation tasks into the list of project activities, as shown in Figure 50.

Figure 49. Project Persistor: expected documentation budget in a development project

No.	Work packages for release 5.0					
No.	Package	Budget	Priority	Responsible	Remark	Release
1	**Functionality**					
1.1	Manual unlocking	2	C	RS	unclear if really needed	5.0
1.2	API typechecking	5	B	AK		5.0
1.3	Improved error codes		A			
2	**Tests**					
2.1	Test cases for caching mechanisms	2	A	RS		5.0
2.2	Java test drivers for all use cases	5	A	CW		5.0
3	**Performance**					
3.1	Performance tuning mechanisms	20	B	RS		5.0 or later
4	**Documentation**					
4.1	Usage concept: describe additional functionality	2	A	AR		5.0
4.2	Usage concept: add example for the state model	1	A	AR		5.0
4.3	Design concept: updates	5	C			5.0 or later
5	**Coaching**					
5.1	Workshop 2000-05-25	5	A	AR		

Figure 50. Project Persistor: project planning sheet including documentation tasks

Project Persistor: documentation as a normal project task

The team met regularly for short status meetings in which the next steps were discussed. Documentation was addressed during these meetings, like all other project tasks. At the beginning, the project had defined certain documents that had to be written, and had decided on a few additional documents later. During the regular meetings the team checked the documents' status and what still needed to be done.

Documents were considered project artefacts just like code, test cases and so on. For each document one person was in charge. Each document had a budget that could be extended on demand and if necessary, but it was clear from the start approximately how much time the project was willing to spend on each document. Figure 50 shows an excerpt from the project planning sheet.

How did the team manage to estimate the effort that was necessary for documentation? This was done mostly based on experience. Figure 49 shows how, in this organisation, the development effort is typically distributed over the various stages of a project, based on the experience of previous projects (Siedersleben 2003). Figure 49 also shows how much of the effort the team expected to go into documentation – proportionately more during the specification stage but diminishing thereafter. The percentage for documentation may seem quite high, and indeed it is smaller in many projects, but the fact that the team was going to build a framework required a comprehensive usage concept, and this justified a larger effort for documentation.

The people who wrote the documents learned a lot in the process. For example, writing the framework's usage concept forced the framework developers to see their framework from a different viewpoint. The authors gained insight into their own system during the writing. Committing a clear concept to paper of how to apply the framework in practical cases forced them to reflect on issues that had gone unnoticed in the design discussions, and that they perhaps had taken for granted.

Unfortunately, the design document wasn't managed so well. The design document lost the team's attention when the team became very busy with other things. The problem wasn't that updates to this document were delayed, it was that from some point on nobody felt responsible for the document, so the necessary updates were never made. Different people added material, but in an uncoordinated way. The document ended up inconsistent and outdated, providing some design ideas but lacking the motivation behind the design and the pros and cons of different approaches that had been discussed. This document didn't serve its purpose very well.

The team decided what documentation was necessary and adjusted their decisions regularly. Overall, this process worked quite well. The document-ation in its entirety was broken down into manageable packages, and each document had ONE RESPONSIBLE AUTHOR and a deadline that would allow for a REVIEW BEFORE DELIVERY.

The documentation of Project Persistor faced one major problem, however. Although it had begun as CONTINUING DOCUMENTATION, updates to the docu-mentation were later neglected when deadlines drew closer and bustling activity set in. As a consequence, the documents' accuracy suffered. Instead of describing how the framework's design had evolved and why, all the design document mentioned were the design ideas the team had had at the beginning of the project.

This was not much of a problem at first, but the team paid for these short-comings two years later when a major refactoring became necessary, as the DESIGN RATIONALE was not available. (See also the project report in Chapter 1, *Project Persistor: difficulties with changed requirements*, page 58.) Browsing outdated documents, the team had a hard time working out the reasoning behind the design changes made during the past two years, and got stuck in dead ends already explored by their colleagues.

I think the important conclusion to draw from this experience is that as far as updating your documents is concerned, you cannot wait until an accurate version is actually needed. This is the moment at which it's too late. Often enough, updates to the documentation are not the most urgent thing a project has to do. But don't confuse *urgent* with *important*. Waiting a little while for documentation updates may be justified – just don't wait until the experts have left the project or are busy with other things.

The experiences of Project Vista back up this view (page 186). The fact that this project performed CONTINUING DOCUMENTATION was the key to its success. Not that the application landscape it produced was accurate all the time – it wasn't. But as the team learned more and more about the applications in the customer's organisation and how they interrelated, they updated the applica-tion landscape, which always mirrored the current understanding and iterated towards an accurate description.

As far as planning the documentation is concerned, we should also look at Project OpenDoors. The documentation in this project lacked THE BIG PICTURE, and overlapping documents didn't exactly present FOCUSED INFORMA-

Project Vista: regular updates to the application landscape

The diagram with the application landscape (Figure 7, page 54) was updated after each interview the consulting team had with the customer. In this way, the diagram always reflected the current knowledge the team had of the application landscape they were to analyse.

This was important, because the diagram was regularly used in interviews to get discussions started. It was given to various customer representatives, who were asked to comment on it, and to add the applications they knew of, as well as the dependencies between applications. By keeping the diagram up to date, the team could make sure that each interview brought additional insight.

Because the diagram had been used successfully during the project, the team felt that a similar technique might be used in other projects as well. The application landscape diagram was presented to the software company's general staff in an article that appeared in the company's quarterly in-house journal. This article briefly introduced the project, and explained the role the diagram had played in the specification of the application landscape. Moreover, the specification (which consisted of essentially that diagram) became part of the software company's repository of exemplary documents for consultancy projects.

TION. (See also the project report in Chapter 1, *Project OpenDoors: communicating the design*, page 55.) This was mainly caused by a problem with the documentation management in this project: most of the documents did not have ONE RESPONSIBLE AUTHOR. Instead, different people added material to the project documentation in a rather uncoordinated way. Overlapping documents and inconsistent information were the consequence, as well as an unnecessary effort spent on too many documents. It was not only the documents that overlapped. The documentation mirrored the overlapping and inconsistent design ideas that were represented in the architecture of the Web portal.

Things changed for the better when a major refactoring occurred. Not only was the software refactored, the documents were as well. This could happen only because at this stage documentation was considered A DISTINCT ACTIVITY. The refactored documents turned out well because each had ONE RESPONSIBLE AUTHOR, who cared for the documentation quality.

Circulating documents

Looking at the reports from Projects Persistor, Vista and OpenDoors, we notice that careful planning alone isn't enough to produce documentation that is useful and that is used. The documents that were used heavily have in

Project OpenDoors: circulating the documentation for feedback

This project involved many teams. The framework team extended a framework that provided the basic functionality for the customer's web portal. Other teams worked on the applications that were going to be integrated into the portal. Because so many teams were involved, and because the teams were under time pressures, the designs of the different applications evolved in slightly different directions. The overall architecture of the web portal thereby became somewhat inconsistent.

Interestingly, there was a similar effect on the documentation. The documentation went a little awry when a number of people worked on different concept papers that addressed overlapping topics. Some of these documents were updated, others weren't, and as a result the documentation became inconsistent in places.

At some point, the architects decided it was time for a refactoring, so that all applications would share a common architecture. During this refactoring, documentation was also addressed. A small group took care of a new set of documents that on one hand described the overall architecture and the design principles, and on the other how the various applications were integrated and how they could be deployed to the Web. These documents underwent an informal review process. Informal though it was, it gave people from several departments an opportunity to share their thoughts. The documentation was reviewed within the framework team and was circulated among the application developers, which included many colleagues from the customer's staff.

Because the concept papers were distributed before the actual coding, the teams who were to use the future versions of the framework could examine these concepts in advance. They learned about what they could expect, but also had the chance to comment on the design concepts. Several weak spots were identified as many other people offered their views.

As a result, both the overall architecture and its documentation were improved. More than that, circulating the documents and asking for feedback contributed to the sense of unity between all parties involved: the IT company, a sub-contractor and the customer. Everybody had been involved, although in different ways.

common that they were actively distributed among the team and to the customer.

There are two sides to this. First, you can distribute a document for a review. A manifest REVIEW CULTURE adds greatly to customer participation and allows teams to receive much feedback on what they have written. Projects Persistor and OpenDoors received a lot of useful feedback when the framework documentation was passed to the framework users. Project Vista learned a lot from discussing the application landscape and what was still missing from it with many of the stakeholders in the customer's organisation. None of these reviews went through a heavyweight process, and the fact that bureaucracy could be avoided contributed much to the review's successes.

Project Extricate, however, provides a warning. While a CUSTOMER REVIEW can be extremely useful, it must be clear to the customer that the document under review is indeed a draft. Project Extricate entered a critical situation when documents were distributed that had not undergone a REVIEW BEFORE DELIVERY and the customer falsely assumed these documents were final.

Project Extricate: problems with unreviewed material

At one point, the team was asked to make a tentative version of the re-engineering concept paper available. This document was important for the customer, and since the customer relationship was good, the team agreed to hand out the preliminary document even though it hadn't been reviewed internally.

Unfortunately, due to some earlier misunderstandings of the application domain, the document contained a few mistakes that hadn't been corrected. When this document was distributed to one of the customer's departments, several people were upset at these mistakes, as they felt they weren't understood. The tentative document version had caused more trouble than good.

The team decided that they would make future versions available only after they had been internally reviewed. These internal reviews never became bureaucratic procedures, but they ensured that serious mistakes in the documentation could be fixed before they could cause unnecessary embarrassment.

The second aspect of the distribution of documents is to emphasise that whoever writes a document is in charge of contacting the TARGET READERS. There's no point in storing a document somewhere, even in its appropriate place, and waiting for others to read it. You stand a much better chance of reaching your readers if you contact them actively and create an INFORMATION MARKETPLACE. In Project Persistor, the team invited the framework users via e-mail to look at the documentation before workshops were held. Project OpenDoors distributed the architecture description actively among the team. Project Vista took a copy of their application landscape diagram to all meetings.

Gaining and preserving knowledge

One good reason for producing a document is to provide an opportunity to think a topic through. This happened in Project Persistor (see the experience report on page 184). The team had had many whiteboard discussions, from which a good idea of the overall architecture had emerged. But when the team committed their design ideas to paper, they were forced to dig deeper. A process of WRITING AND REFLECTION allowed them to think their ideas through and to check for possible inconsistencies of details. Documentation allowed the team to fine-tune the design.

My experience is that this approach works much better for some people than for others. Some people have good ideas in front of a whiteboard, others have excellent thoughts when documenting. The observation is that more introvert people tend to be more creative during writing, while more extrovert people more often than not prefer working with a whiteboard. Since some people learn a lot during a process of WRITING AND REFLECTION, it is wise to retain this opportunity.

Project FlexiCar: keeping the expertise within the company

The designers had chosen an architecture based on an application server, and using EJBs (Enterprise Java Beans) to implement the optimum scheduling of production steps for car manufacturing. The design document that described this architecture evolved along with the software. The document was maintained over the course of the project, which ensured that software and documentation never really got out of sync. Simultaneously, the users of the document provided feedback both on the actual design description and on what was described.

By the time that the project was completed, the design document described the architecture very accurately, including a discussion of the pros and cons of the chosen technological approach. At this point, this document became useful beyond the actual project. The document became part of the company's repository for design documentation, so that other projects in different application domains could profit from the experiences gained with application servers and EJBs.

Once we have acquired the knowledge that's essential for a project, how do we deal with it? The knowledge needs to be shared among the team. Documentation is one way to express knowledge. Direct interaction, for example through discussions and workshops, is another. I've mentioned before that a combination of both is the best strategy for making the collected wisdom of a team available to all members. The more you actively offer the project documents to the intended audience in an INFORMATION MARKETPLACE, the more you'll reach your readers.

The role of documentation isn't restricted to single projects, however. Alistair Cockburn mentions that one important role of documentation is to 'prepare for the next game' (Cockburn 2001). So you need to identify the documents that may be useful beyond the limits of your current project, and make those documents more widely available.

Several project reports give examples of how this can be done. The projects FlexiCar, AirView and Persistor all contributed to the software company's knowledge base – a Web-based information pool that hosts exemplary concept papers and experience reports from earlier projects.

Project AirView: making knowledge on GUI design available

This project was unique in the sense that it focused so much on the GUI design. The design involved ergonomic aspects that weren't normally found in the software company's typical projects.

The company keeps a repository of successful specifications and designs that originate from different projects. The aim is to make experience available company-wide for other project teams to study and, if possible, to reuse. The documents are made available through an intranet. Colleagues can search this intranet for documents that are relevant to a particular technology or to a particular application domain.

The documentation of the GUI design was added to that repository, so that future GUI projects could profit from the experience gained, especially with GUI ergonomics. The documentation was also used as exemplary material in an in-house seminar on specification, in which more experienced software engineers passed on their knowledge to younger colleagues.

Project Vista also contributed to that knowledge base, and in addition became the subject for an article in the software organisation's in-house journal, as described in the project report on page 186.

Obviously, not all project documents are candidates for an organisation's KNOWLEDGE MANAGEMENT. However, when a team keeps a FOCUS ON LONG-TERM RELEVANCE as far as documentation is concerned, the chances are that some documents may be useful in future contexts as well. Documents that describe the DESIGN RATIONALE are particularly useful – the discussion of the pros and cons of different approaches is exactly what will be most useful for future projects.

Project Persistor: feeding the organisation's knowledge base

The documentation included a description of the special versioning technique the data access layer used – two-dimensional versioning (Figure 21 on page 89). This is a rather specialised technique, but it is fairly common for information storage and retrieval in the financial industry. Once the concept had been understood, it was clear that other projects could profit from the expertise as well.

One team member produced an introductory paper for the organisation's knowledge base. This paper explained the basics of two-dimensional versioning and used the same examples as had the framework's usage concept. This paper could be produced with relatively little effort, as most of the material was readily available. Several colleagues used this paper as an information source when they were assigned a project in which two-dimensional versioning played a role.

Finally, Project Contentis demonstrates that KNOWLEDGE MANAGEMENT isn't only about collecting information, but also about retrieving and using it. This project was able to deliver a result much more quickly because the team could rely on experiences from previous projects – a nice example of how useful documentation can be in the long term.

Project Contentis: collected knowledge of CMS requirements

This project had a rather short time frame in which the team had to come up with a list of requirements for a Web content management system.

The team could profit from the fact that their organisation had done consulting on Web content management systems before, and that expertise was already available. Within days, the team had several example requirement lists from previous projects in their hands.

These lists couldn't be used verbatim, of course, since the requirements had to be tailored to the customer's specific needs. Indeed – and not unexpectedly – what used up most of the time in the project was to figure out what those specific requirements were.

Nevertheless, the requirements lists from the previous projects were helpful, as the team didn't have to start from scratch, but could draw on existing material. Alternately, once the project was completed, a new list on requirements could be added to the organisation's knowledge base.

Final Remarks

Now that you have come this far, what are the next steps? You have read the patterns on agile documentation, or at least some of them, and have probably taken a look at the experience reports from the projects in which the patterns were used. The question now is, what can you do to actually improve the documentation processes and the documentation products in your project?

In his book on *Agile Software Development*, Alistair Cockburn recommends: 'Consider agile as an attitude, not a formula'. He goes on: 'In that frame of mind, look at your current project and ask, "How can we, in this situation, work in an agile way?"' (Cockburn 2001).

I think this approach is as viable for agile documentation as it is for agile software development, and I recommend you take this approach when you plan to apply agile documentation in your project. After you have made yourself familiar with the overall ideas of agile documentation, you can look at your project and see how the documentation can be done with an agile *attitude*.

At this point, I'd like to recollect the principles of agile documentation.

> Project documentation is most effective when it is lightweight, without any unnecessary documents, yet providing all the information relevant to readers.

More documentation isn't always better than less. Long documents aren't always better than short ones. An agile project gives preference to lightweight documentation. Look for the topics you feel must be addressed in written documents. Ensure that these documents are written, and written well, but try to do without further documentation. Focus on the right materials.

Documents that are considered necessary can only prove useful if they are of high quality: accurate, up-to-date, highly readable and legible, concise and well structured.

Once you have decided that a document is necessary, don't produce that document half-heartedly. The document can serve its purpose well only if it is accurate and well organised. Straightforwardness will do your documents good.

Tools and techniques are useful only if they facilitate the production of high-quality documents and make their organisation and maintenance easier.

Take an unbiased approach to tools. Tools are supposed to help you in your job, and documentation is no exception. If tools make the documentation in your project harder, do without them. Keep in mind that relatively simple techniques are often sufficient to produce useful documentation.

The documentation process must be efficient and straightforward, must adapt to the requirements of the individual project and must be able to respond to change.

Don't define a complex process for documentation. Alistair Cockburn writes: '*Agile* implies being effective and manoeuvrable. An *agile* process is both light and sufficient' (Cockburn 2001). Just take the steps that are necessary: ensure that good documentation is written, by the right people, and with reasonable effort, but don't make plans beyond that point.

How can you start?

Start small. Starting small is much more promising than trying to achieve everything at a time, as Mary Lynn Manns and Linda Rising point out when they recommend the introduction of new ideas *Step by Step* (Manns Rising 2003).

Start with a few patterns from this book that you feel you can apply in your project easily. The patterns about structuring individual documents, for example, can often be applied immediately. Other things, such as establishing processes, may take a bit longer, but don't require too great an effort either.

Integrate these patterns into your everyday work in an incremental fashion. If you have identified a pattern that you would like to use, the links to related patterns tell you what other issues you might want to consider. In this way you can build up a culture of agile documentation, an attitude of preparing documents in such a way that they are useful for others, your customers and your colleagues alike.

Applying the patterns for agile documentation is rewarding in the sense that your readers will appreciate and profit from your work more. Agile documentation encourages you to do without some of the paperwork found in more heavyweight projects, but makes sure that the effort that you do place on your documents pays off well. You'll be amply repaid by the efficiency of communication in your project.

Pattern Thumbnails

Finding the Right Topics

Target Readers

How can the project team ensure that the documents they produce will be appreciated?

First and foremost, each document must have a target readership, and must address these readers in order to prove useful.

Focused Information

How can documents be prevented from meandering and getting nowhere fast?

A clear and identifiable focus on a particular topic makes a document concise and straightforward. The straightforward document offers the information relevant to this topic, but no more than that.

Individual Documentation Requirements

How can unnecessary documentation requirements be avoided?

The most effective approach towards documentation is for each project to define its documentation requirements individually.

Documentation Portfolio

How can teams reuse the knowledge about which documents might be required in their projects?

A documentation portfolio describes which documents might be necessary in a software project, and their scope. If an organisation sets up such a portfolio, projects can choose those documents they need, checking the necessity of each candidate document individually.

Focus on Long-Term Relevance

How can projects avoid producing documentation that expires too soon?

There is much value in documentation that focuses on issues with a long-term relevance – issues that will play a role in a later project phase or in future projects.

Specification as a Joint Effort

How can development projects ensure that they head in the direction the customer wants?

Every development project requires a specification, which reflects the requirement analysis done jointly by the project team and the customer.

Design Rationale

How can the team make sure that the foundations are laid for future design changes?

Design documents become a valuable source of information if they aren't restricted to describing the actual design, but also focus on the rationale behind the design and explain why the particular design was chosen.

The Big Picture

How can people be introduced to a project without being confronted with a deluge of technical details?

A good feel for a project is best conveyed through a description of the 'big picture' of the architecture that underlies the system under construction.

Separation of Description and Evaluation

How can authors prevent loss of credibility?

Authors gain credibility if, in their documents, they clearly separate description from evaluation.

Realistic Examples

How can abstract material be explained in a comprehensible way?

Project documents are much more convincing if they include realistic examples from the project's context.

Structuring Individual Documents

Structured Information

How can information be presented in an easily accessible way?

Most project documents are best organised as sequential yet well-structured text. This begins with well-chosen chapters and sections, but may well extend to using textual building blocks consistently throughout a document.

Judicious Diagrams

How can authors provide an overview of structures and processes in a convenient way?

Diagrams can provide excellent overviews, while an accompanying text explains details to the extent that is necessary.

Unambiguous Tables

How can authors present systematic information in a precise way?

Tables offer a compact format for the concise and unambiguous presentation of information.

Guidelines for Readers

How can potential readers be informed whether they should read a document, and if so, on which parts they should focus?

Some brief guidelines at the beginning of each document can inform potential readers of the purpose the document serves and explain how different groups of readers should approach the document.

Thumbnail Sketches

How can readers get an overview of the topics dealt with in a document?

Thumbnail sketches provide brief descriptions of the sections of a document, including the section's general goals, as well as its major ideas.

Traceable References

How can documents be linked to each other?

A document should include references to other documents only if readers can obtain those documents without much effort.

Glossary

How can authors make sure that readers understand the vocabulary used in a document?

A glossary can explain technical terms as well as the terms specific to the application domain.

Document History

How can confusion be avoided between versions of a document?

A document history can explain the differences to previous versions of a document, and can relate the document to versions of the software it describes.

Layout and Typography

Text on 50% of a Page

How much space on a page should be devoted to text?

About 50% of the page should be devoted to text.

Two Alphabets per Line

What is the optimum line width?

Approximately two lowercase alphabets of the standard typeface should fit on one line.

120% Line Spacing

What is the optimum line spacing?

The best line spacing is roughly 120% of the type size.

Two Typefaces

How many typefaces are appropriate, and which?

In most cases, two typefaces per document are appropriate – a serif typeface for the body text and a sans-serif typeface for the headings.

Careful Use of Type Variations

How can parts of a text be emphasised?

Type variations can be used for emphasis, but they should be used with care.

Careful Ruling and Shading

How can table cells be separated?

Careful ruling and shading leads to highly legible tables.

Adjacent Placement

How can tables and diagrams be integrated into text?

Diagrams and tables are best placed close to the text from which they are referenced.

Coherent Pages

What options exist to avoid awkward pagination that tears related information apart?

The reading flow is supported by coherent pages – pages that make sure a minimum of related information appears on either side of a page break.

Infrastructure and Technical Organisation

Document Landscape

How can team members get a good overview of what documentation exists in a project?

The project documentation can be represented as a kind of landscape that team members can use as a mental map when they retrieve or add information. A document landscape that roughly forms a tree suits human intuition best.

Document Archive

How can projects avoid the loss of any document versions?

Archiving project documentation offers the advantage that versions can be retrieved when necessary.

Wiki

How can documentation be given a more interactive edge?

A Wiki offers access to the project documentation via an intranet server, and in addition allows the team to post notes and messages to others as necessary.

Code-Comment Proximity

What is an easy way to maintain documentation that refers to the actual code?

Documentation of the code, to the extent that a project team considers it necessary, is best done through source code comments. Separate documents should be reserved for higher-level issues such as overviews, requirements, design and architecture.

Reader-Friendly Media

Which is more appropriate: documents intended for on-line use, or documents intended for print?

The choice of a medium must reflect a document's typical usage. The rule of thumb is: print is good for reading, on-line is good for looking things up.

Separation of Contents and Layout

How can the layouts of text documents be changed and reused easily?

Layout styles can be defined and assigned to content portions. These layout styles can easily be changed and can be reused across documents.

Single Source and Multiple Targets	*How can multiple views of a document be created without doubling maintenance?* The documentation infrastructure can employ mechanisms that take source documents and automatically generate additional views. Such mechanisms avoid double maintenance and ensure consistency.
Import by Reference	*How can different documents use the same diagram or table consistently?* Artefacts that need to appear in multiple contexts can be imported by reference into the documents that include them.
Separation of Processing and Printing	*How can projects produce useful, printable documents?* If a team chooses to deliver the project documentation in a print format that is widely available, all readers are able to print the documents, independent of the platform they use.
Document Templates	*How can all project documents acquire a reasonable structure and a good layout at little cost?* Document templates, once they have been properly designed, impose their structure and layout on all documents that are produced using them.
Few Tools	*How can projects minimise the effort spent on the introduction and use of documentation tools?* Almost all projects can manage with a small set of documentation tools.
Annotated Changes	*How can authors avoid confusion over changes they have made?* While a document is under development, authors can use automatic annotations to identify those parts of the document that have changed recently.
Notification upon Update	*How can readers be prevented from using outdated versions?* Whenever there is a significant change in a project document, all potential readers should be notified of the new version. The notification should roughly explain what has been changed, but should not include the updated material itself.

Reorganisation upon Request

How can the documentation infrastructure be maintained?

Frequent reorganisation makes things worse, not better. Reorganisation of the documentation infrastructure should take place only when it is actively requested by the members of the project team.

Management and Quality Assurance

A Distinct Activity

How should resources be assigned to documentation activities?

When documentation is considered a distinct project activity, and not just the by-product of coding, it can be assigned its own budget, priority and schedule. Documentation can then be weighed against other project activities.

One Responsible Author

How many people should be responsible for a document?

For each project document, there must be one person who accepts responsibility for it. This person need not write the document alone, but must coordinate the contributions from other people.

Continuing Documentation

When should project documentation be written?

Project documentation, when it evolves continuously as the project goes on, offers the advantage that it reflects the last stable state of the project.

Writing and Reflection

How can documentation and other project activities stimulate each other?

To get the best out of documentation, team members have to spend time on the actual writing, as well as in reflection on what they have written, preferably in an undisturbed environment.

Review Culture

How can the quality of the project documents be improved?

Documentation can profit a lot from reviews, provided a review culture has been established in which both authors and reviewers feel comfortable.

Review Before Delivery

How can authors receive the right feedback at the right time?

Early reviews are fine as they help the author shape the scope and the structure of a document. But before a document is officially distributed, or delivered to the customer, a review is mandatory.

Customer Review	*How can a team use documentation to increase customer involvement?*
	Customer reviews can improve the quality of a document, especially as far as the domain expertise is concerned, and at the same time add to team building and integration.
A Distant View	*How can authors obtain unbiased feedback?*
	Authors can obtain unbiased feedback from reviewers who are interested in the topic and who are generally knowledgeable in the field, but who are not involved in the actual work described in the document.
Information Marketplace	*How can good documents be prevented from going sadly unnoticed?*
	Documents gain more attention if the intended readers are actively invited to read them.
Knowledge Management	*How can future projects profit from a successful project?*
	Only when project documentation is made available organisation-wide do future projects have a chance of drawing on the expertise gained.

Glossary

Agile Alliance

A group of 17 people who first met in February 2001 with the aim of finding better ways of developing software. The *authors* of the *Agile Manifesto*.

See www.AgileAlliance.org.

Agile development

Software development following the principles expressed in the *Agile Manifesto*.

Agile Manifesto

A collection of core values and principles intended to lead to better ways of software development, as defined by the *Agile Alliance*.

See www.AgileManifesto.org.

Agile process

Any process – specifying, modelling, designing, coding or other process – that follows the principles expressed in the *Agile Manifesto*.

Author

For the purposes of this book, anyone who writes a project *document*. Typically this is a team member who also has other tasks. Hardly ever a professional technical writer.

CASE

Computer-aided software engineering, as in 'CASE tool'.

Class diagram

A *UML* diagram that shows classes, their attributes and their operations, as well as various static relationships that exist between these classes such as association, aggregation and inheritance.

Content

The actual text of a *document*, independent of *layout* or formatting.

Cookbook

A *document* that explains how to use a software system through step-by-step advice.

Deliverable

Any artefact that a project is supposed to deliver to the customer. This can include source code, executable software and *documents*.

Design document

A *document* that describes how the software is organised internally and why it is organised that way. Typically, a design document describes how software is composed from smaller parts and how these parts are related. *Class diagrams* and *interaction diagrams* are often the method of choice to describe a design.

Document

A persistent artefact that is set up specifically to provide information in writing. A document is typically produced electronically, and can be read either as a printed copy or on-line.

Documentation

The entirety of *documents* and source code comments produced in a project. Also the process that comprises the collection, classification and dissemination of information.

Document processing

The process of creating, editing, changing, maintaining and printing *documents*, as is typically done with a *word processor*.

Font

The set of characters belonging to a certain *typeface* of a given size.

HTML

Hypertext Markup Language. A language used to define the appearance and behaviour of pages when displayed in a Web browser. HTML allows the definition of text blocks as well as the definition of hyperlinks.

Hypertext

Text organised in a non-sequential way with hyperlinks providing access from one chunk of information to others. Typically, multiple access paths allow *readers* to travel through a hypertext in different ways.

Interaction diagram

A *UML* diagram that visualises the message passing between collaborating objects.

Layout

The set of characteristics that define a *document's* visual appearance.

Legibility

The degree to which a printed page can be recognised quickly and reliably. The legibility mainly depends on how well *readers* can identify the characters of the *typeface* used.

Meta-information

In the context of *documentation*, a chunk of text or a group of keywords that provide information about the *document's* status and the type of information it contains.

On-line document

A *document* that is intended to be read with the use of a Web browser or other viewing application. Often access to the document is given through the Internet or an in-house intranet, but the document may also be located on the local computer. On-line documents may have hyperlinks by which documents can be linked.

Paragraph format

A specification that defines the formatting properties for all paragraphs of a given type within a *document*, as used in a *word processor*.

PDF

Portable Document Format – an electronic *document* format developed by Adobe Systems Inc. that is portable between different computer types, designed for on-line viewing, but now also used as a *print format*.

PostScript

A *document* description language designed to be a *print format* portable between printing devices.

Print document

A *document* intended for printing, as opposed to an *on-line document*.

Print format

A specification that describes exactly how a *document* will appear when printed. Examples include *PDF* and *PostScript*.

Readability

The degree to which a text can easily be grasped and understood by the *reader*.

Reader

A person who uses a *document* to obtain information at an arbitrary level of detail. This includes not only those who read a document from beginning to end, but also occasional readers who browse through a document in search for specific information.

Refactoring

Reorganisation of a software system without changing its external behaviour, with the aim of improving its internal structure. When applied to documentation: improving the project documentation's structure without changing its contents.

Review

The process of having a *document* checked by someone other than the *author*, typically with the intention of improving the document's quality with regard to *contents*, structure and language.

Software project

A project the goal of which is in some way related to software development. This may be a development project in which the *deliverables* are items of software, or it may be a consultancy project that is still concerned with software development, although in a less direct way.

Specification document

A *document* that describes what a software product is supposed to do. A specification document defines the requirements placed on the software.

Template

An artefact that is not itself a *document*, but specifies the *layout* and the formatting for a class of similar documents. Most *word processors* support the use of document templates.

Thumbnail

A brief summary of a longer text.

Tutorial

A *document* that explains how to use a software system.

Typeface

A collection of characters, including letters, digits and symbols, intended for the visual display of language and all designed in a similar style. Examples include Times, Helvetica, Garamond and Frutiger. Most typefaces are designed as families and include sets of characters for different *type sizes*, as well as variations such as boldface, italics and small caps.

Type size

The size of a *typeface*, normally measured in points. A typical range of type sizes suitable for printed *documents* is 8–24 points.

Typography

The science, craft or art of setting up a printed page. Typography deals with letters, diagrams, lines, area and colour.

UML

Unified Modeling Language.

UP

Unified Process.

Use case

A sequence of actions to be performed with a software system that, as a whole, represent a typical usage scenario.

Word processor

For the purposes of this book, a tool for *document processing*. Word processors cover varying degrees of complexity, ranging from simple text editors to sophisticated desktop publishing systems.

References

Alexander Ishikawa Silverstein 1977

> Christopher Alexander, Sara Ishikawa, Murray Silverstein: *A Pattern Language – Towns • Buildings • Construction*, Oxford University Press, New York, 1977.

Alexander 1979

> Christopher Alexander: *The Timeless Way Of Building*, Oxford University Press, New York, 1979.

Ambler 2002

> Scott W. Ambler: *Agile Modeling – Effective Practices for eXtreme Programming and the Unified Process*, John Wiley & Sons, 2002.

Beck Cunningham 1989

> Kent Beck, Ward Cunningham: 'A Laboratory for Teaching Object-Oriented Thinking', in *Proceedings of OOPSLA '89*, ACM Press, 1989.

Beck 2000

> Kent Beck: *Extreme Programming Explained: Embrace Change*, Addison-Wesley, 2000.

Berczuk Appelton 2003

> Steve Berczuk, Brad Appelton: *Software Configuration Management Patterns: Effective Teamwork, Practical Integration*, Addison-Wesley, 2003.

Berleant 2000

> Daniel Berleant: 'Does Typography Affect Proposal Assessment', in *Communications of the ACM*, Vol. 43, No. 8, August 2000.

Botafogo Rivlin Shneiderman 1992

Rodrigo A. Botafogo, Ehud Rivlin, Ben Shneiderman: 'Structural Analysis of Hypertexts: Identifying Hierarchies and Useful Metrics', in *ACM Transactions on Information Systems*, Vol. 10, No. 2, April 1992.

Brand 1999

Stewart Brand: *The Clock of the Long Now – Time and Responsibility*, Basic Books, New York, 1999.

Brooks 1995

Frederick P. Brooks: *The Mythical Man-Month*, Addison-Wesley, Anniversary Edition, 1995.

Buschmann Meunier Rohnert Sommerlad Stal 1996

Frank Buschmann, Regine Meunier, Hans Rohnert, Peter Sommerlad, Michael Stal: *Pattern-Oriented Software Architecture – A System of Patterns*, John Wiley & Sons, 1996.

Cockburn 1998

Alistair Cockburn: *Surviving Object-Oriented Projects – A Manager's Guide*, Addison-Wesley, 1998.

Cockburn 2000

Alistair Cockburn: *Writing Effective Use Cases*, Addison-Wesley, 2000.

Cockburn 2001

Alistair Cockburn: *Agile Software Development*, Addison-Wesley, 2001.

Conover 1985

Theodore E. Conover: *Graphic Communications Today*, West Publishing Company, 1985.

Coplien 1995

James O. Coplien: 'A Generative Development-Process Pattern Language', in *Pattern Languages of Program Design*, Vol. 1, James O. Coplien, Douglas C. Schmidt (Eds.), Addison-Wesley, 1995.

Coplien 2000

James O. Coplien: 'A Pattern Language for Writers' Workshops', in *Pattern Languages of Program Design,* Vol. 4, Neil Harrison, Brian Foote, Hans Rohnert (Eds.), Addison-Wesley, 2000.

Crowder 1982

Robert G. Crowder: *The Psychology of Reading*, Oxford University Press, 1982.

DeMarco Lister 1987

Tom DeMarco, Timothy Lister: *Peopleware: Productive Projects and Teams*, Dorset House, 1987. (2nd Edition, Dorset House, 1999.)

Dumais 1988

Susan T. Dumais: 'Textual Information Retrieval,' in *Handbook of Human-Computer Interaction*, Elsevier (North-Holland), 1988.

EuroPLoP 1998

Jens Coldewey, Paul Dyson (Eds.): *Proceedings of the 3rd European Conference on Pattern Languages of Programs, 1998*, Universitätsverlag Konstanz.

EuroPLoP 1999

Paul Dyson, Martine Devos (Eds.): *Proceedings of the 4th European Conference on Pattern Languages of Programs, 1999*, Universitätsverlag Konstanz.

EuroPLoP 2000

Martine Devos, Andreas Rüping (Eds.): *Proceedings of the 5th European Conference on Pattern Languages of Programs, 2000*, Universitätsverlag Konstanz.

EuroPLoP 2001

Andreas Rüping, Jutta Eckstein, Christa Schwanninger (Eds.): *Proceedings of the 6th European Conference on Pattern Languages of Programs, 2001*, Universitätsverlag Konstanz.

Flanagan 2002

David Flanagan: *Java in a Nutshell*, O'Reilly & Associates, 2002.

Fowler 1996

Martin Fowler: *Analysis Patterns*, Addison-Wesley, 1996.

Fowler 2000

Martin Fowler: *UML Distilled*, 2nd Edition, Addison-Wesley, 2000.

Furnas Zacks 1994

> George W. Furnas, Jeff Zacks: 'Multitrees: Enriching and Reusing Hierarchical Structure', in *CHI '94 – Conference Proceedings on Human factors in Computing Systems*, ACM, 1994.

Gabriel 2002

> Richard Gabriel: *Writers' Workshops and the Work of Making Things: Patterns, Poetry ...* Addison-Wesley, 2002.

Gamma Helm Johnson Vlissides 1995

> Erich Gamma, Richard Helm, Ralph Johnson, John Vlissides: *Design Patterns: Elements of Reusable Object-Oriented Software*, Addison-Wesley, 1995.

Glasser 1992

> Theodore L. Glasser: 'Objectivity and News Bias,' in *Philosophical Issues in Journalism*, Elliot D. Cohen (Ed.), Oxford University Press, 1992.

Gulbins Kahrmann 1992

> Jürgen Gulbins, Christine Kahrmann: *Mut zur Typographie*, Springer, 1992. (German language)

Haramundanis 1998

> Katherine Haramundanis, *The Art of Technical Documentation*, Butterworth-Heinemann, 1998.

Harrison 1996

> Neil B. Harrison: 'Organizational Patterns for Teams', in *Pattern Languages of Program Design*, Vol. 2, John M. Vlissides, James O. Coplien, Norman L. Kerth (Eds.), Addison-Wesley, 1996.

Harrison 2000

> Neil B. Harrison: 'The Pattern Language of Shepherding', in *Pattern Languages of Program Design*, Vol. 4, Neil Harrison, Brian Foote, Hans Rohnert (Eds.), Addison-Wesley, 2000.

Highsmith 2000

> Jim Highsmith: *Adaptive Software Development*, Dorset House, 2000.

Highsmith 2002

> Jim Highsmith: *Agile Software Development Ecosystems*, Addison-Wesley, 2002.

Horn 1989

Robert E. Horn: *Mapping Hypertext*, Lexington Institute, 1989.

Horton 1994

William Horton: *Designing and Writing Online Documentation*, John Wiley & Sons, 2nd Edition, 1994.

Hsu Mitchell 1997

Richard C. Hsu, William E. Mitchell: 'After 400 Years, Print is Still Superior', in *Communications of the ACM*, Vol. 40, No. 10, October 1997.

Jacobsen Booch Rumbaugh 1999

Ivar Jacobsen, Grady Booch, James Rumbaugh: *The Unified Software Development Process*, Addison-Wesley, 1999.

Kerth 2001

Norman Kerth: *Project Retrospectives: A Handbook for Team Reviews*, Dorset House, 2001.

Knuth 1992

Donald E. Knuth: *Literate Programming*, Center for the Study of Language and Information, 1992.

Kruchten 2000

Philippe Kruchten: *The Rational Unified Process*, Addison-Wesley, 2000.

Leuf Cunningham 2001

Bo Leuf, Ward Cunningham: *The Wiki Way*, Addison-Wesley, 2001.

Manns Rising 2003

Mary Lynn Manns, Linda Rising: *Fear Less and Other Patterns for Introducing New Ideas into Organizations*, 2003 (in preparation).

Miller 1956

George A. Miller: 'The Magical Number Seven, Plus or Minus Two: Some Limits on our Capacity for Processing Information', in *The Psychological Review*, Vol. 63, No. 2, American Psychological Association, March 1956.

Nielsen 2000

Jakob Nielsen: *Designing Web Usability – The Practice of Simplicity*, New Riders Publishing, 2000.

Noble Weir 2000

> James Noble, Charles Weir: *Small Memory Software*, Addison-Wesley, 2000.

Orenstein 1996

> Robert Orenstein: 'A Pattern Language for an Essay-Based Web Site', in *Pattern Languages of Program Design*, Vol. 2, John M. Vlissides, James O. Coplien, Norman L. Kerth (Eds.), Addison-Wesley, 1996.

Pinker 1997

> Steven Pinker: *How the Mind Works*, Allen Lane, The Penguin Press, 1997.

PLoPD 1995

> James O. Coplien, Douglas C. Schmidt (Eds.): *Pattern Languages of Program Design*, Vol. 1, Addison-Wesley, 1995.

PLoPD 1996

> John M. Vlissides, James O. Coplien, Norman L. Kerth (Eds.): *Pattern Languages of Program Design*, Vol. 2, Addison-Wesley, 1996.

PLoPD 1998

> Robert C. Martin, Dirk Riehle, Frank Buschmann (Eds.): *Pattern Languages of Program Design*, Vol. 3, Addison-Wesley, 1998.

PLoPD 2000

> Neil Harrison, Brian Foote, Hans Rohnert (Eds.): *Pattern Languages of Program Design*, Vol. 4, Addison-Wesley, 2000.

Parnas 1972

> David Parnas: 'On the Criteria to be Used in Decomposing Systems into Modules', in *Communications of the ACM*, Vol. 15, No. 2, December 1972.

Poppendieck 2003

> Mary Poppendieck: *Lean Development – An Agile Toolkit for Software Development Managers*, 2003 (in preparation).

Press 2000

> Larry Press: 'From P-books to E-books', in *Communications of the ACM*, Vol. 43, No. 5, May 2000.

Rising 2000a

Linda Rising: 'Customer Interaction Patterns', in *Pattern Languages of Program Design*, Vol. 4, Neil Harrison, Brian Foote, Hans Rohnert (Eds.), Addison-Wesley, 2000.

Rising 2000b

Linda Rising: *The Patterns Almanac 2000*, Addison-Wesley, 2000.

Rumbaugh Jacobsen Booch 1998

James Rumbaugh, Ivar Jacobsen, Grady Booch: *The Unified Modeling Language Reference Manual*, Addison-Wesley, 1998.

Rüping 1998a

Andreas Rüping: 'The Structure and Layout of Technical Documents', in *Proceedings of the 3rd European Conference on Pattern Languages of Programming and Computing 1998*, Jens Coldewey, Paul Dyson (Eds.), Universitätsverlag Konstanz.

Rüping 1998b

Andreas Rüping: 'Writing and Reviewing Technical Documents', in *Proceedings of the 3rd European Conference on Pattern Languages of Programming and Computing 1998*, Jens Coldewey, Paul Dyson (Eds.), Universitätsverlag Konstanz.

Rüping 1999a

Andreas Rüping: 'Project Documentation Management', in *Proceedings of the 4th European Conference on Pattern Languages of Programming and Computing 1999*, Paul Dyson, Martine Devos (Eds.), Universitätsverlag Konstanz.

Rüping 1999b

Andreas Rüping: 'Typography and Desktop Publishing', in *Proceedings of the 4th European Conference on Pattern Languages of Programming and Computing 1999*, Paul Dyson, Martine Devos (Eds.), Universitätsverlag Konstanz.

Salton 1989

Gerard Salton: *Automatic Text Processing – The Transformation, Analysis, and Retrieval of Information by Computer*, Addison-Wesley, 1989.

Schmidt Stal Rohnert Buschmann 2000

Douglas Schmidt, Michael Stal, Hans Rohnert, Frank Buschmann: *Pattern-Oriented Software Architecture 2 – Patterns for Concurrent and Networked Objects*, John Wiley & Sons, 2000.

Schneider 1996

Wolf Schneider: *Deutsch für Kenner – Die neue Stilkunde*, Piper, 1996. (German language)

Schneider 1999

Wolf Schneider: *Deutsch für Profis – Wege zu gutem Stil*, Goldmann, 1999. (German language)

Schwaber Beedle 2001

Ken Schwaber, Mike Beedle: *Agile Software Development with Scrum*, Prentice Hall, 2001.

Siedersleben 2003

Johannes Siedersleben (Eds.): *Softwaretechnik*, Hanser, 2003. (German language)

Sommerville 1996

Ian Sommerville: *Software Engineering*, Addison-Wesley, 1996.

Strunk White 1979

William Strunk, E. B. White: *The Elements of Style*, Macmillan, 3rd edition, 1979.

Tinker 1963

Miles A. Tinker: *Legibility of Print*, Iowa State University Press, 1963.

Tufte 1997

Edward R. Tufte: *Visual Explanations: Images and Quantities, Evidence and Narrative*, Graphics Press, 1997.

Tufte 2001

Edward R. Tufte: *The Visual Display of Quantitative Information*, Graphics Press, 2nd Edition, 2001.

Völter Schmid Wolff 2002

Markus Völter, Alexander Schmid, Eberhard Wolff: *Server Component Patterns – Component Infrastructures Illustrated With EJB*, John Wiley & Sons, 2002.

Weinberg 1998

Gerald M. Weinberg: *The Psychology of Computer Programming*, Silver Anniversary Edition, Dorset House, 1998.

Weir 1997

Charles Weir: 'Patterns for Designing in Teams: How Teams Can Improve the Design Process', in *Pattern Languages of Program Design*, Vol. 3, Robert C. Martin, Dirk Riehle, Frank Buschmann (Eds.), Addison-Wesley, 1997.

West 1990

Suzanne West: *Working with Style: Traditional and Modern Approaches to Layout and Typography*, Watson Guptill, 1990.

Index